Monographs
*of the*
*American Jewish Archives*
Number 11

*Jacob R. Marcus*
*and Abraham J. Peck*
*Editors*

# Monographs of the American Jewish Archives

1. *Jewish Americana* (1954)
2. *An American Jewish Bibliography* by Allan E. Levine (1959)
3. *Reference to Jews in the Newport Mercury, 1758-1786* by Irwin S. Rhodes (1961)
4. *The Theology of Isaac Mayer Wise* by Andrew F. Key (1962)
5. *Manual of the American Jewish Archives* by David M. Zielonka (1966)
6. *Selected Items of American Jewish Interest in the Yiddish Periodicals of Russia and Poland, 1862-1940* by Leo Shpall (1966)
7. *Commerce and Contraband in New Orleans during the French and Indian War* by A. P. Nasatir and James R. Mills (1968)
8. *The Jews of Coro, Venezuela* by Isaac S. Emmanuel (1973)
9. *A Century of Memories: The East European Jewish Experience in America* edited by Uri D. Herscher (1982)
10. *Among the Survivors of the Holocaust—1945 The Landsberg DP Camp Letters of Major Irving Heymont, United States Army* (1982)
11. *The Jewish Experience. A Guide to Manuscript Sources in the Library of Congress* compiled by Gary J. Kohn (1986)

# THE JEWISH EXPERIENCE

## A Guide to Manuscript Sources in the Library of Congress

*Compiled by*
GARY J. KOHN

AMERICAN JEWISH ARCHIVES
On the Cincinnati Campus
of the
Hebrew Union College—Jewish Institute of Religion
1986

COPYRIGHT © 1986
AMERICAN JEWISH ARCHIVES

**Library of Congress Cataloging-in-Publication Data**

Kohn, Gary J.
  The Jewish experience.

  (Monographs of the American Jewish Archives ; 11)
  Bibliography: p.
  Includes index.
  1. Jews—United States—Archival resources—United
States—Washington (D.C.)—Directories.
2. Jews—History—Archival resources—Washington (D.C.)
—Directories.  3. Library of Congress—Directories.
4. Manuscripts—Washington (D.C.)—Directories.  I. Title.
II. Series.
Z6373.U5K64   1986      [E184.J5]     016.973'04924    86-17305
ISBN 0-87820-014-2

Manufactured in the United States of America

# CONTENTS

| | |
|---|---:|
| Introduction | ix |
| Acknowledgments | xiii |
| I. COLLECTIONS | 1 |
| II. INDIVIDUALS AND CORPORATIONS | 19 |
|    A. Individuals | 19 |
|    B. Corporations | 74 |
|       1. Institutions | 74 |
|       2. Organizations | 76 |
|       3. Publications | 85 |
| III. SUBJECTS | 87 |
|    A. Americana | 87 |
|    B. Israel | 92 |
|       1. Middle East | 92 |
|       2. Palestine | 107 |
|       3. Zionism | 113 |
|       4. Miscellany | 116 |
|    C. Judaica | 121 |
|       1. Biblical | 121 |
|       2. Literature | 122 |
|       3. Music | 122 |
|       4. Religion | 123 |
|    D. Miscellany | 124 |
|    E. Persecution | 128 |
|       1. Anti-Semitism | 128 |
|       2. Holocaust | 132 |
|          a. Concentration Camps | 132 |
|          b. Eichmann, Adolph | 134 |
|          c. Hitler, Adolf | 134 |
|          d. Refugees | 136 |

|       |    |                      |     |
|-------|----|----------------------|-----|
|       | e. | War Crimes and Trials | 139 |
|       | f. | Warsaw Ghetto        | 142 |
|       | g. | Miscellany           | 142 |
| 3.    | Inquisition |               | 147 |
| 4.    | Russian/Soviet Jewry |       | 148 |
| 5.    | Miscellany  |               |     |

Index     151

# DEDICATION

To those heroes and martyrs whose accomplishments and sufferings form the basis of this book. May their legacy enable my wife Niki and me to raise our son Ari and our daughter Dena Sara to live without fear of war or famine, hatred or disease.

# INTRODUCTION

With approximately 10,000 collections and 50 million items in its custody, the holdings of the Manuscript Division of the Library of Congress are among the largest in the world. Much of the material pertains to various phases of American history, from the precolonial era to the present.

While it is common knowledge that the history of the Jewish people in America has mirrored that of America itself, it is less well known that the Manuscript Division's collections reflect that image. From a seventeenth-century transcript of an Inquisition trial in Mexico to Haym Salomon and the Revolutionary War, and from Judah Benjamin and the Confederate States of America to Henry Kissinger and the Arab-Israeli conflict, the national collection contains vast amounts of material which should not be ignored as important sources for studies of the Jewish experience in the United States and its impact upon American and world history.

One of the most frustrating aspects of conducting historical research is often the inability to determine the location of relevant subject matter. That this limitation applies to sources for American Jewish history in particular and Jewish history in general is no exception, particularly with respect to those materials in the Manuscript Division of the Library of Congress.

*The Jewish Experience* attempts to remedy this shortcoming. It is a compilation of as comprehensive a list of sources as possible in the Manuscript Division pertaining to the study of Jewish history. The need for such a guide exists because of the nature of the organization of the Manuscript Division's collections. The system is organized around an alphabetical list of collections by names of individuals or organizations, supplemented by finding aids and other reference tools. In addition, there are subject and item-by-item indexes which are less comprehensive. Consequently, research is often not only very time-consuming, but also so cumbersome so as to discourage and prevent scholars from discovering the rich, but hidden, wealth within the Manuscript Division's collections.

## CRITERIA

The criteria used to compile the "individuals" and "collections" sections of this guide were the same as those used by the compilers of the *Encyclopaedia Judaica*. Specifically, so long as a person was born a Jew he is Jewish for the purposes of this guide, even if he subsequently converted or otherwise denounced his heritage. Once Jewish identity was established, editorial judgments were made in determining whether a person was significant enough to include in the "individuals" section.

Subject categories were chosen on the basis of the observation of general topics reflective of the content of the collections and of a sustained historical interest not only of Jewish history in the Americas, but worldwide as well.

## LIMITATIONS

As previously stated, a major obstacle in compiling this guide was the limited nature of the Manuscript Division's indexing system. Compounding the problem was the fact that even where particular collections may have been arranged on an item-by-item or subject matter basis, because of a lack of particular interest of either the collector or the processor, the true content of the collection may not have been accurately reflected in its description. Added to the inherent problems of verification of Jewish identity, these obstacles were bound to affect the content of this guide.

## HOW TO USE THE GUIDE

The guide is divided into three parts, each of which is independent of the others, all of which, however, should be surveyed by the thorough scholar.

The "collections" section is composed of entries of collection titles within the Manuscript Division of Jewish individuals or organizations, while the "individuals and corporations" section consists of an index of prominent Jewish individuals and corporate entities represented by materials scattered throughout various collections in the Division's custody. Main entries in the "subjects" section are arranged alphabetically by collection title within various subject headings, with subheadings providing information on the subject in question.

The following are examples, with accompanying explanations, of typical entries within each of the three sections of the guide.

INTRODUCTION xi

*Collections section*

```
      1           2
      ↓           ↓
*BERNAYS, EDWARD L. (1891-    ) ← 3
4 → Papers (1897-1965) ← 5           8 →  200,000 items
    Public relations  ← 6            9 →  120 ft.
    NUCMC 67-0588.  ← 7             10 →  F
```

  1. Access. Those entries marked with an asterisk (*) indicate that there is a restriction on access to that collection. The reader should contact the Manuscript Division as to the nature of that restriction.
  2. Collection title
  3. Birth and death dates
  4. Type of material
  5. Span dates of collection
  6. Occupation
  7. *National Union Catalog of Manuscript Collections* entry number
  8. Collection size by number of items
  9. Collection size in linear feet
  10. Finding aid, register, or index is available

*Individuals and Corporations section*

```
         1                         3              4
         ↓                         ↓              ↓
BERNAYS, EDWARD L. (1891-    ) ← 2  U.S. public relations executive
26 ← 6           Ackerman, Carl W. ← 5
          7 → *Bernays, Edward L.
```

  1. Name of individual
  2. Birth and death dates
  3. Country of most recent citizenship
  4. Occupation
  5. Title of the collection in which information on the individual can be found
  6. Container numbers, and occasionally folder headings, have been supplied, where possible to determine, for the convenience of scholars. It is important to point out, however, that collections are constantly being reorganized, and container numbers may therefore change. Scholars should also be cautioned not to limit their search to the containers cited, as further relevant material may be found by exploring other portions of the collection.
  7. Access restricted

Subjects section

1 → *BERNAYS, EDWARD L. ← 2
3 → 13                    4 → Jewish affairs, 1945 ← 5

1. Access restricted
2. Collection title
3. Container number
4. Subject entry within the collection
5. Span dates of the entry

Because the "subjects" section is arranged according to the collection title in which the relevant material is located, and because there may be occasional cases where different portions of the same topics are covered by more than one subject heading, the researcher is encouraged to consult all pertinent areas of possible coverage.

All dates, occupations, and labels as to the content of collections in both type of material and amount were taken from the records of the Manuscript Division and are a product of its cataloging system, except for the dates in the "individuals" section, which were obtained from various biographical sources.

The Jewish Experience is concerned only with those manuscript materials which are in the custody of the Manuscript Division of the Library of Congress. It is important to note, however, that other kinds of manuscript materials relevant to Jewish studies exist elsewhere within the Library, most notably in the Hebraic Section, the Music Division, and the Rare Book and Special Collections Division.

# ACKNOWLEDGMENTS

The completion of this guide could not have been accomplished without the assistance and cooperation of the staff of the Manuscript Division. In particular, I would like to thank John McDonough, whose encouragement and guidance during the initial stages of my research were invaluable.

Equally deserving of thanks for his guidance and inspiration is Myron Weinstein, former Head of the Hebraic Section of the Library of Congress, and for her untiring assistance, Phyllis H. Weisbard, another former employee of that office.

# I. COLLECTIONS

**ADLER, ALFRED** (1870-1937)
    Family papers (1888-1970)    750 items
    U.S. psychologist, psychiatrist    1.6 ft.
    F

*****ARENDT, HANNAH** (1906-1975)
    Papers (1898-1976)    28,000 items
    U.S. philosopher, political scientist, educator    30 ft.
    NUCMC 80-2028    F

**BAKST, LEON N.** (1866-1924)
    Collection (1923)    3 items
    Russian artist    .1 ft.

**BEER, GEORGE LOUIS** (1872-1920)
    Diary (1919)    1 item
    U.S. diplomat, historian    .1 ft.

**BELMONT, AUGUST** (1816-1890)
    Collection    5 items
    U.S. banker, diplomat    .1 ft.

**BENJAMIN, JUDAH P.** (1811-1894)
    Collection (1827-1871)    7 items
    U.S. Senator, Secretary of War of Confederate States    .1 ft.
        of America, attorney

**BENSASSON, MAURICE JACQUES** (   -   )
    Letter (1929)    1 item
    .1 ft.

**BERLINER, EMILE** (1851-1929)
    Papers (1856-1929)      19 items
    U.S. Inventor      .4 ft.

**\*BERNAYS, EDWARD L.** (1891-    )
    Papers (1897-1965)      200,000 items
    Public realtions      120 ft.
    NUCMC 67-0588      F

**\*BERNFELD, SIEGFRIED** (1892-1953)
    Papers (1854-1970)      6,000 items
    Psychoanalyst      9.2 ft.
    NUCMC 77-1492      F

**BEYER, OTTO STERNOFF** (1868-1948)
    Papers (1915-1948)      35,000 items
    Engineer, economist, labor leader      53 ft.
    NUCMC 59-0236      F

**\*BOORSTIN, DANIEL J.** (1914-    )
    Papers
    U.S. historian, Librarian of Congress

**\*BORNSTEIN, BERTA** (    -1971)
    Papers      15,000 items
    U.S. Psychoanalyst      37.5 ft.

**BRANDEIS, LOUIS DEMBITZ** (1856-1941)
    Letters (1926-1941      4 items
    U.S. lawyer, jurist, Zionist leader      .1 ft.

**\*BREUER, JOSEF** (1842-1925)
    Collection (1880-1960)      100 items
    Austrian physician, physiologist, psychoanalyst      .1 ft.

**CELLER, EMANUEL** (1888-1981)
    Papers (1924-1972)      183,000 items
    U.S. lawyer, Congressman      214.8 ft.
    NUCMC 70-0942      F

**COHEN, ALBERT MORRIS** (1883-1959)
    Papers (1904-1959)      200 items
    U.S. naval officer      .8 ft.
    NUCMC 71-1344

**\*COHEN, BEN V.** (1894-1983)
    Papers      6,500 items
    U.S. presidential advisor, lawyer      10.4 ft.
         F

**COMMONER, BARRY** (1917-    )
    Papers
    U.S. biologist

**CONFERENCE ON NEAR EASTERN AFFAIRS** (1922-23: Lausanne, Switzerland)
    Records (1922-23)      1 item
         .4 ft.

**DANIEL GUGGENHEIM FUND**
    Records (1926–1943)      6,000 items
    Promotion of aeronautics      8 ft.
    NUCMC 62-2697      F

**DAVIDSON, JO** (1883-1952)
    Papers (1906-1952)      5,400 items
    U.S. sculptor, artist      7.2 ft.
         F

**DISRAELI, BENJAMIN** (Beaconsfield, 1st Earl of) (1804-1881)
    Collection      15 items
    Prime Minister of Britain, author      .1 ft.

**DREIKURS, RUDOLPH** (1897-1972)
    Papers (1911-1972)      5,500 items
    Psychiatrist, educator      14.8 ft.
    NUCMC 76-0154      F

**EINSTEIN, ALBERT** (1879-1955)
    Papers (1916-1949)                                                      40 items
    Physicist, Zionist leader                                  .4 ft.
    NUCMC 79-1775

**ETZIONI, AMITAI W.** (1929-    )
    Papers
    U.S. educator, sociologist

**EVARTS (EPSTEIN), LILLIAN** (1910-1960)
    Papers (1933-1956)                                          8,400 items
    U.S. Poet                                                         21 ft.

**\*FEDERN, PAUL** (1871-1950)
    Papers (1872-1950)                                          6,000 items
    Psychoanalyst                                                2.8 ft.
                                                                          F

**FEINBERG, CHARLES COLLECTIONS**
    **SHAPIRO, KARL**
        Collection (1963-1968)                              170 items
                                                                          6 ft.
                                                                          F

    **WHITMAN, WALT**
        Collection                                               11,000 items
                                                                           83 ft.
                                                                          F

**\*FEIS, HERBERT** (1893-1972)
    Papers (    -1972)                                            36,500 items
    U.S. economist, historian, writer           50.8 ft.
                                                                           F

**FERBER, EDNA** (1887-1968)
    Letter                                                                 1 item
    U.S. author                                                          .1 ft.

**FEUCHTWANGER, LION** (1884-1958)
    Literary manuscript      1 item
    German author      .4 ft.

**FINE, REUBEN** (   -   )
    Chess scores (1931-1941)      475 items
    U.S. Chess player      .4 ft.

**\*FLEXNER, ABRAHAM** (1866-1959)
    Papers (1870-1955)      12,000 items
    U.S. author, educator      10.5 ft.
    NUCMC 66-1404      F

**FRANKFURTER, FELIX** (1882-1965)
    Papers (1864-1965)      70,000 items
    U.S. lawyer, educator, Zionist leader, juror      106.2 ft.
    NUCMC 68-2033      F

**\*FREUD, ANNA** (1895-1982)
    Papers (1954-1969)
    British psychoanalyst

**\*FREUD, HARRY** (1909-1968)
    Papers (1850-1969)
    U.S. businessman; nephew of Sigmund Freud

**\*FREUD, SIGMUND** (1856-1939)
    Collection (1851-1956)      9,000 items
    Austrian psychiatrist      22.4 ft.
         F

**FRIEDENWALD, HARRY** (1864-1950)
    Collection (1933-1935)      6 items
    U.S. Author      .1 ft.

**\*GARMENT, LEONARD** (1924-   )
    Papers (1969-1974)      7,000 items
    U.S. Lawyer, government official      4.4 ft.
         F

**\*GERTZ, ELMER** (1906-        )
    Papers                                                               243,000 items
    U.S. lawyer, writer, collector            269.6 ft.
                                                                                  F

**GIIELSON, MAXWELL** (1902-1965)
    Papers (1918-1965)                        25,000 items
    U.S. psychiatrist, psychologist          43 ft.
    NUCMC 67-0607                                   F

**GOLDENWEISER, EMANUEL A.** (1883-1953)
    Papers (1919-1952)                          1,500 items
    U.S. economist                                    3 ft.
    NUCMC 59-0027                                   F

**GOLDMARK, PAULINE D.** (1873-1962)
    Papers (1865-1941)                             16 items
    U.S. social worker                             .1 ft.

**GOLDSBOROUGH, LOUIS M.**
    Papers (1817-1874)                           8,000 items
    U.S. naval officer                               16 ft.

**GOMPERS, SAMUEL** (1850-1924)
    Miscellaneous Manuscript Collection     1 item
        Signature                                           .1 ft.
    American Federation of Labor
        Letterbooks (1883-1925)              172,000 items
    U.S. labor leader                                84 ft.
    NUCMC 67-0583                                   F

**GOUDSMIT, SAMUEL ABRAHAM** (1902-        )
    Collection (1940-1947)                     300 items
    Physicist, editor                                .4 ft.
    NUCMC 72-1720

**GRATZ, BENJAMIN** (1791-1883)
    Papers                                                               2 items
    U.S. merchant, philanthropist              .1 ft.

**GRATZ, REBECCA** (1781-1869)
    Collection      48 items
    U.S. philanthropist      .1 ft.

**GRUENBERG, BENJAMIN C. & SIDONIE M.** (1881-1974)
    Papers (1878-1974)      28,000 items
    U.S. child specialists, writers, educators      55.6 ft.
    F

**GUGGENHEIM, HARRY F.** (1890-1971)
    Papers (1918-1934)      1,200 items
    U.S. Philanthropist      3 ft.
    F

**GUITERMAN, ARTHUR** (1871-1943)
    Collection (1936-1941)      111 items
    U.S. poet      .1 ft.

**HAYES, ISAAC ISRAEL** (1832-1881)
    Autograph      1 item
    U.S. Physician, explorer      .1 ft.

**HECHT, BEN** (1894-    )
    Autobiography (1954)      1 item
    U.S. dramatist, playwright      .4 ft.

**HELLMAN, LILLIAN** (1905-1984)
    Playscript      1 item
    U.S. dramatist      .1 ft.

**HERTZ, EMANUEL** (1870-1936)
    Collection (1826-1936)      80 items
    U.S. jurist      2 ft.
    NUCMC 67-0610

**HOSTOVSKY, EGON** (1908-1973)
    Papers (1934-1969)      1,000 items
    U.S. Author      1.2 ft.

**HUEBSCH, BENJAMIN W.** (1876-1964)
    Papers (1893-1964)                   20,515 items
    U.S. Publisher                      17 ft.
    NUCMC 66-1421                   F

**ISAKOWER, OTTO** (1899-    )
    Papers                           2,700 items
    Psychiatrist, psychoanalyst      2 ft.
                                   F

**JUDAH, HENRY MOSES** (1821-1866)
    Journal (1864)                   1 item
    U.S. Army officer             .4 ft.
    NUCMC 79-1793

**KAGAN, SOLOMON ROBERT** (1881-1955)
    Papers (1910-1952)           109 items
    U.S. Physician, author       .1 ft.

**KANIN, GARSON** (1912-    )
    Papers (1941-1964)          2,500 items
    U.S. playwright, director    6 ft.
    NUCMC 73-0897                  F

**KATZ, JOSEPH** (1888-1958)
    Autograph collection         32 items
    U.S. Collector, advertising executive   .1 ft.

**KAUFMAN, GEORGE SIMON** (1889-1961)
    Plays (1911-1941)            350 items
    U.S. playwright                .8 ft.
    NUCMC 80-2058

**\*KISSINGER, HENRY A.** (1923-    )
    Papers
    U.S. educator, government official

**KLEIN, JULIUS** (1901-    )
    Collection (1960-1965)     27 items
    U.S. Army officer, journalist, publisher     .1 ft.

**KRAUS, HANS P.** (1907-    )
    Collection—Spanish-American Documents     300 items
       (1500-1819)     4.4 ft.
    U.S. Rare book collector, publisher     F
    NUCMC 70-0955

**KRAUS, KARL** (1874-1936)
    Literary manuscript (1926)     1 item
    German Author     .4 ft.

**KROLL, JACK** (1885-1971)
    Papers (1927-1968)     3,600 items
    U.S. Labor executive     7.5 ft.
    NUCMC 71-1372     F

**\*KUBIE, LAWRENCE S.** (1896-1973)
    Papers (1943-1979)     30,000 items
    U.S. Psychoanalyst, Physician     75 ft.

**LANGMUIR, IRVING** (1881-1957)
    Papers (1871-1957)     32,000 items
    U.S. inventor, chemist     42.7 ft.
    NUCMC 71-1374     F

**LASKI, HAROLD J.** (1893-1950)
    Letter     1 item
    British political scientist, educator     .1 ft.

**LEHMAN, HERBERT H.** (1878-1963)
    Letter (1939)     1 item
    U.S. banker, Governor of New York     .1 ft.

**LERNER, ABBA PTACHYA** (1903-1982)
    Papers (1929-1982)     15,000 items
    U.S. Economist, professor     37.5 ft.

**LEVENTHAL, HAROLD** (1915-1979)
    Papers (1956-1979)                          65,750 items
    U.S. Jurist                                     164.3 ft.

**LEVY, URIAH PHILLIPS** (1792-1862)
    Collection (1842-1857)                      2 items
    U.S. naval officer                             .1 ft.

**LIPMANN, FRITZ ALBERT** (1899-    )
    Papers (1970)                                  2 items
    U.S. Biochemist                               .4 ft.

**LOEB, JACQUES** (1859-1924)
    Papers (1889-1924)                         11,000 items
    U.S. Physiologist, educator            24 ft.
    NUCMC 74-1069                              F

**LUDWIG, EMIL** (1881-1948)
    Papers (1941)                                  1 item
    Swiss Historian, writer                   .4 ft.

**MADOL, HANS R. (GERHARD SALOMON)** (1903-1956)
    Diaries (1935-48)                             7 items
    British Historian, public official      1.2 ft.

**\*MALAMUD, BERNARD** (1914-1986)
    Papers (1952-1969)                         110 items
    U.S. writer                                     6 ft.

**MARX, GROUCHO** (1895-1977)
    Papers                                          352 items
    U.S. comedian, actor                      2 ft.

**MARX, KARL** (1818-1883)
    Collection (1873)                             1 item
    German philosopher, writer, founder of     .1 ft.
        Communism

## MEIER, NELLIE SIMMONS (1862-1944)
    Collection      500 items  
    U.S. collector of handprints      1.2 ft.  
    F

## MEYER, EUGENE (1875-1959)
    Papers (1910-1938)      110,000 items  
    U.S. news executive      69 ft.  
    F

## MORDECAI, ALFRED (1804-1887)
    Papers (1790-1946)      3,700 items  
    U.S. Army officer, engineer      6.8 ft.

## *MORGENTHAU, HANS, J. (1904-1980)
    Papers      80,000 items  
    U.S. Political scientist, educator, author      81.8 ft.  
    F

## MORGENTHAU, HENRY SR. (1856-1946)
    Papers (1834-1940)      36,000 items  
    U.S. businessman, diplomat, ambassador      23.8 ft.  
    NUCMC 60-0124      F

## MOSES, RAPHAEL JACOB (1812-1893)
    Papers (1890-1975)      3 items  
    U.S. lawyer, soldier, politician      .4 ft.  
    NUCMC 80-2072

## *MOUNT, CHARLES M. (1928-    )
    Papers  
    U.S. artist, art historian

## NATIONAL COUNCIL OF JEWISH WOMEN—NATIONAL OFFICE
    Records (1911-1980)      40,000 items  
     100 ft.

## NATIONAL COUNCIL OF JEWISH WOMEN—WASHINGTON, D.C. OFFICE
    Records (1944-1969)      530.4 ft.
     F

## NEUFELD, MAURICE F. (1910-   )
    Papers      2,000 items
    U.S. Labor leader, educator, author      2.8 ft.
    NUCMC 59-0009      F

## *NIEDERLAND, WILLIAM G. (1904-   )
    Papers
    Psychiatrist, psychoanalyst

## NIZER, LOUIS (1902-   )
    Manuscripts (1961)      2,000 items
    U.S. lawyer, author      2 ft.

## ODETS, CLIFFORD (1906-1963)
    Plays (1934-1938)      3 items
    U.S. dramatist      .4 ft.

## OPPENHEIMER, J. ROBERT (1904-1967)
    Papers (1921-1980)      74,000 items
    U.S. Physicist, public official      122 ft.
    NUCMC 71-1392      F

## PERTSCHUK, MICHAEL (1933-   )
    Papers (1977-1983)      54,000 items
    U.S. Public Official, lawyer      135 ft.

## PHILLIPS, PHILIP FAMILY (1807-1884)
    Family papers (1832-1914)      7,000 items
    U.S. lawyers      8.8 ft.
    NUCMC 62-4557      F

**PINCUS, GREGORY** (1903-1967)
    Papers (1920-1927)
    U.S. Biologist

43,000 items
85.2 ft.
F

**\*PODHORETZ, NORMAN** (1930-    )
    Papers
    U.S. author, critic, editor

8,000 items
11 ft.
F

**PULITZER, JOSEPH** (1847-1911)
    Papers (1870-1924)
    U.S. Journalist, publisher
    NUCMC 67-0629

5,500 items
5 ft.
F

**RAPAPORT, DAVID** (1911-1960)
    Papers (1939-1960)
    U.S. Psychoanalyst
    NUCMC 63-0390

106,000 items
31.2 ft.
F

**\*RIBICOFF, ABRAHAM A.** (1910-    )
    Papers (1949-1980)
    U.S. Senator, public official

235,000 items
262.8 ft.
F

**ROSENTHAL, ALBERT** (1863-1939)
    Collection (1897)
    U.S. Artist

2 items
.1 ft.

**ROSENWALD, LESSING JULIUS** (1891-1979)
    Papers (1891-1980)
    U.S. merchant, bookman, collector

28,000 items
32.4 ft.
F

**\*ROTH, PHILIP** (1933-    )
    Papers
    U.S. author

1,600 items
16.4 ft.

**ROTHSCHILD, MEYER AMSCHEL** (1773-1855)
    Letter (1836)     1 item
    German financier     .1 ft.

**RUKEYSER, MURIEL** (1913-1980)
    Collection (1941-1979)     30,000 items
    U.S. poet     75 ft.

**SCHWIMMER, ROSIKA** (1877-1948)
    Collection (1930-1948)     15 items
    U.S. Public official, political activist     .1 ft.

**SELZER, MICHAEL I.**
    Collection (1925-1978)     44 items
    U.S. Political scientist     .1 ft.

**SHAPIRO, KARL JAY** (1913-    )
    Papers (1939-1968)     2,300 items
    U.S. poet, editor, educator     5 ft.
    NUCMC 72-1756     F

**SOBELOFF, SIMON E.** (1893-1973)
    Papers (1882-1973)     95,000 items
    U.S. lawyer, public official     158 ft.
         F

**\*SPINGARN, ARTHUR** (1878-1971)
    Papers (1911-1964)     37,000 items
    U.S. lawyer, author, founder of NAACP     30 ft.
    NUCMC 66-1458     F

**\*SPIVAK, LAWRENCE E.** (1900-    )
    Papers (1927-1973)     30,000 items
    U.S. producer, publisher, political analyst     136.8 ft.
    NUCMC 74-1074     F

**STEINHARDT, LAURENCE A.** (1892-1950)
    Papers (1929-1950)     42,000 items
    U.S. lawyer, economist, diplomat     42.6 ft.
    NUCMC 65-0932     F

**STOKES, ROSE HARRIET PASTOR** (1879-1933)
    Collection (1913-1915)      5 items
    U.S. social worker, lecturer, author      .1 ft.

**STRAUS, OSCAR S.** (1850-1926)
    Papers (1856-1920)      37,000 items
    U.S. businessman, diplomat, public official      21.2 ft.
    NUCMC 60-0157      F
    Oscar S. Straus Memorial Association Records      2,500 items
          3.6 ft.
          F

**STRAUSS, JOSEPH** (1861-1948)
    Papers (1881-1922)      25 items
    U.S. Naval officer      .4 ft.
    NUCMC 72-1764

**STRAUSS, LEWIS LICHTENSTEIN** (1896-1974)
    Autograph collection (1749-1885)      12 items
    U.S. Corporate executive, naval officer, public official      .1 ft.

**TELLER, EDWARD** (1908-    )
    Article ("The Legacy of Hiroshima"—1962)      1 item
    U.S. Physicist, author, scientist      .4 ft.

**TOURO, JUDAH** (1775-1854)
    Will      1 item
    U.S. merchant, philanthropist      .1 ft.

**UNITED NATIONS—PALESTINE PARTITION RESOLUTION**
    (1948)      1 item
          .1 ft.

**\*UNTERMEYER, LOUIS** (1885-1977)
    Papers (1915-1967)      425 items
    U.S. poet, author, editor      5.2 ft.
    NUCMC 65-0938      F

**VEBLEN, OSWALD** (1880-1960)
    Papers (1881-1960)      13,600 items
    U.S. Mathematician      17.2 ft.
    NUCMC 78-1767      F

**VON NEUMANN, JOHN** (1903-1957)
    Papers (1938-1957)      18,000 items
    U.S. Mathematician      18 ft.
         F

**WAKSMAN, SELMAN ABRAHAM** (1888-1973)
    Papers (1916-1959)      1,500 items
    U.S. microbiologist      2.8 ft.
    NUCMC 62-4565      F

**WOLF, SIMON** (1836-1923)
    Letter (1917)      1 item
    U.S. lawyer, author      .1 ft.

**WOLMAN, ABEL** (1892-    )
    Papers (1957-1965)      500 items
    U.S. Engineer, educator      33.6 ft.
    NUCMC 66-1464      F

**WOLMAN, LEO** (1890-1961)
    Papers (1914-1958)      15,000 items
    U.S. Economist      15.2 ft.
         F

**WUNDERLICH, GEORGE M.** (1883-1951)
    Papers (1897-1951)      2,700 items
    German Lawyer, educator      4.5 ft.
    NUCMC 59-0221      F

**ZEITLIN, JACOB** (1883-1937)
    Poem      1 item
    U.S. Educator, writer      .1 ft.

**ZOLA, EMILE** (1940-1902)
    Letter (1878)      1 item
    French novelist      .1 ft.

**ZORACH, WILLIAM** (1887-1966)
    Papers (1822-1974)      14,000 items
    U.S. artist, sculptor      20.5 ft.
    NUCMC 63-041      F

**ZWEIG, STEFAN** (1881-1942)
    Papers      1 item
    Austrian Writer      .4 ft.

# II. INDIVIDUALS AND CORPORATIONS

## A. INDIVIDUALS

**AARONSOHN, AARON** (1876-1919)      Israeli statesman, agronomist
1      American Peace Commission to Versailles
125      Frankfurter, Felix
     Frankfurter Zionism Collection
4      Morgenthau, Henry
7      Rosenwald. Lessing J.

**ABZUG, BELLA S.** (1920- )      U.S. Congresswoman, activist, attorney
2      *Podhoretz, Norman

**ADELMAN, KENNETH L.** (1946- )      U.S. government official, political scientist
1      *Podhoretz, Norman

**ADLER, ALFRED** (1870-1937)      U.S. psychologist, psychiatrist
     Adler, Alfred
1-3      American Society of Adlerian Psychology
     Dreikurs, Rudolf
C2, 6      *Mead, Margaret

## ADLER, CYRUS (1863-1940)     U.S. Jewish communal leader, educator, Orientalist

| | |
|---|---|
| 1, 96 | Cattell, James McKeen |
| 20 | Frankfurter, Felix |
| 5 | Morgenthau, Henry M., Sr. |
| | Roosevelt, Theodore |
| 2, 3, 9 | Rosenwald, Lessing J. |
| | Straus, Oscar S. |
| | Taft, William Howard |
| 923 | Washington, Booker T. |
| | Wilson, Woodrow |

## ADLER, FELIX (1851-1933)     U.S. educator, philosopher

| | |
|---|---|
| | Foulke, William D. |
| | Lindsey, Benjamin Barr |
| | Roosevelt, Theodore |
| | Stanton, Elizabeth Cady |
| | Straus, Oscar S. |
| | Taft, William Howard |
| | Traubel, Horace |
| 340 | Washington, Booker T. |
| | Wilson, Woodrow |

## ALINSKY, SAUL (1909-   )     U.S. social activist

| | |
|---|---|
| 1 | Lynd, Robert and Helen |
| 7 | Meyer, Agnes |
| | Wallace, Henry A. |

## ALLON, YIGAL (1918-1980)     Israeli statesman, soldier, public official

| | |
|---|---|
| 246 | Spivak, Lawrence E. |

## ARENDT, HANNAH (1906-1975)     U.S. philosopher, political scientist, educator

| | |
|---|---|
| | *Arendt, Hannah |
| | *Morgenthau, Hans J. |
| 1, 6 | *Podhoretz, Norman |

INDIVIDUALS AND CORPORATIONS 21

**ASCH, SHOLEM** (1880-1957) U.S. author
2 Heubsch, Benjamin W.
 Wallace, Henry A.

**ASIMOV, ISAAC** (1920-    ) U.S. science fiction writer, biochemist
1 *Gamov, Barbara and George

**BARUCH, BERNARD** (1870-1965) U.S. public official, financier, philanthropist
 *Alsop, Joseph and Stewart
Diary Anderson, Chandler P.
10 Arnold, Henry H.
 Baker, Newton D.
85, 101 Baker, Ray Stannard
 Beer, George, Louis
4 Bingham, Robert Worth
4 Bonsal, Stephen
 Bryan, William Jennings
10 Bush, Vannevar
105 Clapper, Raymond
29 *Corcoran, Thomas G.
2 *Cohen, Benjamin V.
4 Creel, George
4 Crosby, Oscar T.
64-65 Daniels, Josephus
 *Davies, Joseph E.
Diary Davis, Norman H.
II-1 *Douglas, William O.
11 *Feis, Herbert
17 *Flexner, Abraham
23 Frankfurter, Felix
 Garfield, Harry A.
 Gregory, Thomas Watt
4 Hagedorn, Hermann
Diary Hamlin, Charles S.
 Harriman, Florence J.
 Howard, Roy
 Hull, Cordell

| | |
|---|---|
| Diary, 46 | Ickes, Harold L. |
| 7 | *Jackson, Robert H. |
| 35-39 | James, Marquis |
| 3 | Jones, Jesse H. |
| 9, 17 | King, Ernest J. |
| | Krug, Julius A. |
| 3 | Land, Emory Scott |
| | Leffingwell, Russell C. |
| | Long, Breckinridge |
| A58, B53 | *Luce, Claire Boothe |
| 1 | *Luce, Henry L. |
| | McCormick, Lynde D. |
| 1 | McGowen, Samuel |
| 5 | McLean, Evelyn Walsh |
| 2 | MacLeish, Archibald |
| 9, 94 | Meyer, Eugene |
| | *Mills, Ogden L. |
| | Morgenthau, Henry Sr. |
| 3 | Mowrer, Edgar and Lillian |
| 62 | Murdock, Victor |
| | Nielson, Fred K. |
| 19 | Oppenheimer, J. Robert |
| | Osborn, Fairfield |
| 1 | Overholser, Winfred |
| | Parsons, William S. |
| 18 | *Patterson, Robert P. |
| | Pershing, John J. |
| | Pittman, Key |
| 11 | Pulitzer, Joseph II |
| | Reid Family |
| | Roosevelt, Theodore |
| 26 | Roosevelt, Theodore Jr. |
| 33 | Russell, Charles Edward |
| 2 | Sullivan, Mark |
| | Sweetser, Arthur |
| | Taft, William Howard |

|  |  |  |
|---|---|---|
| 44, 55 | Tumulty, William | |
|  | Walsh, Thomas J. | |
| 12 | Waterman, Alan J. | |
|  | White, Henry | |
|  | Williams, John Sharp | |
| 9 | Wilson, Edith Bolling | |
|  | Wilson, Woodrow | |
| 2 | Woolley, Robert W. | |

**BEER, GEORGE LOUIS** (1872-1920)　　　　U.S. diplomat, historian
　　　　　　　　Beer, George Louis
59, 171　　　　Jameson, J. Franklin

**BEGIN, MENACHEM** (1913-　　) Israeli soldier, statesman, Prime Minister
4　　　　　　　*Former Members of Congress
　　　　　　　*Ribicoff, Abraham A. (1979)
190　　　　　Spivak, Lawrence E. (1975)

**BELLOW, SAUL** (1915-　　)　　　　　　U.S. writer, educator
1　　　　　　Harrison, Gilbert A.
6　　　　　　Podhoretz, Norman
4　　　　　　*Simpson, Louis A. M.

**BELMONT, AUGUST** (1816-1890)　　　　U.S. banker, diplomat
　　　　　　Bayard, Thomas F.
　　　　　　Belmont, August
　　　　　　Belmont, August
　　　　　　Corcoran, William W.
　　　　　　Marble, Manton M.
　　　　　　Marcy, William L.
　　　　　　Reid Family

**BEN-GURION, DAVID** (1886-1973)　　　Israeli statesman, Prime Minister
501　　　　　Celler, Emanuel
4　　　　　　Denny, George V.
23, 28　　　　Frankfurter, Felix
　　　　　　Klein, Julius
　　　　　　Reid Family
30　　　　　Spivak, Lawrence E.

**BENJAMIN, JUDAH P.** (1811-1884)  U.S. lawyer, Senator,
Secretary of War of Confederate States of America
  Banks, Nathaniel P.
  Barton-Jenifer Families
  Batchelder, John
  Beauregard, P. T. G.
  Benjamin, Judah P.
  Blair, Francis P.
  Burwell, William M.
  Butler, Benjamin B.
  Cameron, Simon
  Causten-Pickett
  Chesnut, James
  Clay, Thomas J.
  Colfax, Schuyler
  Confederate States of America
  Corcoran, William W.
  Crittenden, John J.
  Curry, Jabez L. M.
  Cushing, Caleb
  Dahlgren, John A. B.
  Delano, Columbus
  Early, Jubal A.
  Easby-Smith Family
  Eustis, George
  Fillmore, Millard
  Fish, Hamilton
  Forney, John W.
  Garfield, James A.
  Goodwin, James H.
  Gwinn, William N.
  Hammond, James H.
  Harris, Isham G.
  Harrison, Burton
  Holmes, George F.
  Holt, Joseph
  Hotchkiss, Jedediah
  Hotze, Henry
  Johnson, Reverdy
  Johnston, Albert S.

Johnston, William P.
Lee, Samuel P.
London Exhibition of 1851
Lovell, Mansfield
Mangum, Willie P.
Marcy, William L.
Martin, Letitia B.
Mason, James M.
Maury, Matthew F.
McCook Family
McPherson, Edward
Milton, George F.
Moran, Benjamin
Myer, Albert J.
North, Simeon N.D.
Pecquet, du Bellet Paul
Phillips, Philip
Pickens-Bonham
Pickett, John T.
Pierce, Franklin
Reynolds, Thomas C.
Rives, William C.
Roman, Alfred
Sanders, George N.
Schoolcraft, Henry R.
Selfridge, Thomas O.
Sherman, John
Stanton, Edwin M.
Stephens, Alexander H.
Thompson, Jacob
Trenholm, George A.
Tucker, Nathaniel B.
Tyler, John
U.S. Library of Congress Archives
U.S. Works Progress Administration—Mallory, Stephen R.
Van Dorn, Earl
Wadsworth Family
Walker, Robert J.
Washburne, Elihu B.

                    Welles, Gideon
                    Wheeler, John H.
                    Willis, Edward

**BERENSON, BERNARD** (1865-1959)    U.S. art historian and collector
11           Hay, John
             Loeb, Jacques
             Smith, Logan Pearsall

**BERGSON, PETER** (Kook, Hillel) (1915-   )    Israeli Zionist leader, government official
Diary       Ickes, Harold L.
46          Meyer, Eugene
            Wallace, Henry A.

**BERLIN, IRVING** (1888-   )    U.S. songwriter, music publisher
8            Eaker, Ira C.
1            Gordon, Ruth
            Harriman, Florence J.
3            MacLeish, Archibald
46          Meyer, Eugene
11          Pulitzer, Joseph II
            Reid Family
26          Roosevelt, Theodore Jr.

**BERNAYS, EDWARD L.** (1891-   )    U.S. public relations executive
26          Ackerman, Carl W.
            *Bernays, Edward L.
9            *Federn, Paul
A9          *Freud, Sigmund
C31         *Mead, Margaret
10          Meyer, Eugene
            *Morgenthau, Hans J.
            Mowrer, Edgar and Lillian
36          Nichols, William I.
3            Ogilvy, David

INDIVIDUALS AND CORPORATIONS 27

11 Pulitzer, Joseph II
 Reid Family
22 Roosevelt, Kermit

**BERNFELD, SIEGFRIED** (1892-1953) U.S. psychoanalyst
 *Bernfeld, Siegfried
9 *Federn, Paul
B6 *Freud, Sigmund

**BERNSTEIN, LEONARD** (1918- ) U.S. conductor, composer, musician
2 *Cain, James M.
4 Middleton, George

**BETTELHEIM, BRUNO** (1903- ) U.S. psychologist, educator, author
 Gitelson, Maxwell
 Rapaport, David

**BLOOM, SOL** (1870-1949) U.S. businessman, Congressman
39 Ackerman, Carl
20 American Society of Landscape Architects
 Fitzpatrick, John C.
Diary Ickes, Harold L.
4 Kleine, George
5 McLean, Evalyn Walsh
3 MacLeish, Archibald
11 Meyer, Eugene
 Wallace, Henry A.

**BOAS, FRANZ** (1858-1942) U.S. anthropologist, ethnologist
99 Cattell, James McKeen
 McGee, William J.
B1, M13, 038 *Mead, Margaret
 Newcomb, Simon

**BOHR, NIELS H. D.** (1885-1962) Danish physicist, scientist
12 Bush, Vannevar
127 Frankfurter, Felix

| | |
|---|---|
| 2 | Gamow, George |
| | Langmuir, Irving |
| 20-21 | Oppenheimer, J. Robert |
| 3 | Veblen, Oswald |

**BOORSTIN, DANIEL J.** (1914-    )   U.S. historian, Librarian of Congress

| | |
|---|---|
| | American Scholar |
| | *Bernays, Edward L. |
| | *Boorstin, Daniel J. |
| 2 | *Cohen, Benjamin V. |
| | *Corcoran, Thomas G. |
| 25 | Frankfurter, Felix |
| 1, 5 | Malina, Frank J. |
| C31 | *Mead, Margaret |
| | *Morgenthau, Hans J. |

**BRANDEIS, LOUIS DEMBITZ** (1856-1941)   U.S. Supreme Court Justice, lawyer, Zionist leader

| | |
|---|---|
| C204 | American Council of Learned Societies |
| 86, 102 | Baker, Ray Stannard |
| | Bayard, Thomas F. |
| | Beer, George Luis |
| 5 | Bingham, Robert W. |
| 58 | *Black, Hugo L. |
| | Bonaparte, Charles J. |
| | Brandeis, Louis Dembitz |
| 159 | Carnegie, Andrew |
| 2, 12 | *Cohen, Benjamin V. |
| | *Corcoran, Thomas G. |
| 67 | Daniels, Josephus |
| II-2 | *Douglas, William O. |
| 11-12 | *Feis, Herbert |
| | Fisher, Walter L. |
| | Ford Peace Plan |
| 26-29, 127-28, 224 | Frankfurter, Felix |
| | Frankfurter Zionism Collection |
| | Gregory, Thomas Watt |

## INDIVIDUALS AND CORPORATIONS 29

| | |
|---|---|
| 1 | Goldenweiser, Emanuel A. |
| | Goldmark, Pauline |
| Diaries | Hamlin, Charles |
| 3 | *Holmes, John Haynes |
| 3 | Huebsch, Benjamin W. |
| Diaries | Ickes, Harold L. |
| | *Jackson, Robert |
| A38 | Kingsbury, John A. |
| 4 | Landis, James M. |
| | Lansing, Robert |
| B83 | *La Follette Family |
| | Lindsey, Benjamin Barr |
| | McAdoo, William G. |
| 3 | MacLeish, Archibald |
| 1A | Meyer, Agnes |
| 13, 98 | Meyer, Eugene |
| 5 | Middleton, George |
| 5 | Morgenthau, Henry Sr. |
| 68, 70 | Murdock, Victor |
| IC63 | *NAACP |
| | Pinchot, Amos |
| 434, 449 | Pinchot, Gifford |
| | Redfield, William C. |
| | Richberg, Donald J. |
| | Roosevelt, Theodore |
| | *Spingarn, Arthur |
| 73 | Stone, Harlan Fiske |
| | Sutherland, George |
| | Taft, William Howard |
| | Thompson, Huston |
| | Van Devanter, Willis |
| 1 | Vrooman, Carl Schurz |
| | Walsh, David I. |
| | Warren, Charles |
| | White, William Allen |
| | Whitlock, Brand |
| | Wilson, Woodrow |
| 2 | Woolley, Robert W. |

**BRANT, IRVING** (1885-1976)    U.S. historian, author, editor
19            *Black, Hugo L.
              Brant, Irving N.
47            *Corcoran, Thomas G.
12            Rutledge, Wiley B.
7             Stone, Harlan Fiske
              Wallace, Henry A.

**BRICE, FANNY** (1891-1951)    U.S. comedian, singer
5             McLean, Evalyn Walsh

**BUBER, MARTIN** (1878-1965)    Israeli philosopher, writer, educator
1             *Bernfeld, Siegfried

**BUCHWALD, ART** (1925-    )    U.S. journalist, author
              Mauldin, William
              Reid Family

**CANTOR, EDDIE** (1892-1964)    U.S. entertainer
36            Nichols, William I.
1             Rosenwald, Lessing J.

**CARDOZO, BENJAMIN N.** (1870-1938)    U.S. Supreme Court Justice, lawyer
C178          American Council of Learned Societies
58            *Black, Hugo L.
5             Brant, Irving N.
2             *Brill, Abraham
5             *Cairns, Huntington
115, 126, 129 Frankfurter, Felix
3             *Holmes, John Haynes
Diaries       Ickes, Harold L.
              *Jackson, Robert
4             Landis, James M.
14            Meyer, Eugene
6             *Patterson, Robert P.

INDIVIDUALS AND CORPORATIONS        31

| | |
|---|---|
| 10 | Stephens, Harold M. |
| 8, 74 | Stone, Harlan Fiske |
| | Taft, William Howard |
| | Warren, Charles |

**CELLER, EMANUEL** (1888-1981)        U.S. Congressman, lawyer

| | |
|---|---|
| 5 | Brant, Irving N. |
| | Celler, Emanuel |
| 2 | *Cohen, Benjamin V. |
| 4 | Fahy, Charles |
| | Granik, Samuel T. |
| 4 | MacLeish, Archibald |
| | Mann, Arthur W. |
| | National Woman's Party |
| 6, 30 | *Patterson, Robert P. |
| | Reid Family |
| 123 | Sanger, Margaret |
| C285 | White, William Allen |

**CERF, BENNETT A.** (1898-1971)        U.S. publisher, editor, comedian

| | |
|---|---|
| 7, 10 | Jackson, Shirley |
| | Knox, Dudley, W. |
| | *Louchheim, Katie S. |
| 7 | Moore, Merrill |
| 36-7, 39, 61 | Nichols, William I. |
| | Reid Family |

**COHEN, BEN V.** (1894-1983)        U.S. presidential advisor, lawyer

| | |
|---|---|
| 23 | *Black, Hugo L. |
| | *Cohen, Ben V. |
| | *Corcoran, Thomas G. |
| 4 | Fahy, Charles |
| 45, Zionism | Frankfurter, Felix |
| Diaries | Ickes, Harold L. |
| 9 | *Jackson, Robert H. |
| 4 | *MacLeish, Archibald |
| 45 | Meyer, Eugene |

| | |
|---|---|
| 12 | *Morgenthau, Hans J. |
| 26 | Oppenheimer, J. Robert |
| 2 | Van Doren, Irita B. |
| | Wallace, Henry A. |

**COHEN, WILBUR J.** (1913-    )        U.S. government official, educator
                    Ames, Louise B.
                    Ilg, Frances G.
26               Anderson, Clinton P.
                    *Ribicoff, Abraham A.

**COMMONER, BARRY** (1917-    )        U.S. biologist
                    Commoner, Barry
C67, 76, 85, 88, 110   *Mead, Margaret

**DAVIDSON, JO** (1883-1952)        U.S. sculptor, artist
                    Davidson, Jo
                    *La Follette Family
                    Wallace, Henry A.

**DAYAN, MOSHE** (1915-1981)        Israeli soldier, statesman, author
                    *Kissinger, Henry A.
                    *Osborne, John
234             Spivak, Lawrence E.

**DE HAAS, JACOB** (1872-1937)        U.S. Zionist leader, writer
534             Daniels, Josephus
                    Frankfurter Zionism Collection
                    Wilson, Woodrow

**DE LA MOTTA, JACOB** (1789-1845)        U.S. physician, religious leader
                    Jefferson, Thomas
                    Madison, James

**DISRAELI, BENJAMIN** (1804-1881)        British author, Prime Minister
                    Beaconsfield, Benjamin Disraeli
38              Bryan, William Jennings (9/13/23)
                    Johnson, Reverdy

| | | |
|---|---|---|
| 231 | Long, Breckinridge | |
| 213 | Moore, John Bassett | |
| 55 | NAWSA | |
| 5 | *Podhoretz, Norman | |

**DREYFUS, ALFRED** (1859-1935)        French Army Officer
| | |
|---|---|
| 61 | *Arendt, Hannah |
| 61 | Bell, Alexander Graham |
| 15 | Buneau-Varilla, Phillipe |
| | Cutting, Bronson M. |
| | Harrison, Benjamin |

**DUBINSKY, DAVID** (1892-1982)        U.S. labor leader
| | |
|---|---|
| 11 | Brotherhood of Sleeping Car Porters |
| | *Corcoran, Thomas G. |
| | Frey, Joseph P. |
| Diary | Ickes, Harold L. |
| | National Woman's Party |
| | *Patterson, Robert P. |
| | Reid Family |
| 8 | Rosenwald, Lessing J. |
| | Wallace, Henry A. |
| | White, William Allen |

**EBAN, ABBA** (1915-   )        Israeli statesman, educator, author
| | |
|---|---|
| | Celler, Emanuel |
| 8 | *Cohen, Benjamin V. |
| 6 | Fahy, Charles |
| 52 | Frankfurter, Felix |
| C41 | *Mead, Margaret |
| 9 | Mowrer, Edgar A. |
| | Reid Family |
| 16 | Sobeloff, Simon E. |
| 233, 246 | Spivak, Lawrence E. |
| | Warren, Earl |

## EINSTEIN, ALBERT (1879-1955)    U.S. physicist

| | |
|---|---|
| C264 | American Council of Learned Societies |
| | American Scholar |
| | Batchelder, John D. |
| 17 | *Bernfeld, Siegfried |
| 15 | Cattell, James M. |
| 1 | Chase, Stuart |
| | Commoner, Barry |
| | Einstein, Albert |
| A10, B3, D18 | *Freud, Sigmund |
| 52 | Frankfurter, Felix |
| 3 | Gamov, Barbara and George |
| 2 | *Gertz, Elmer |
| | Hale, George E. |
| | Harriman, Florence J. |
| 7 | Huebsch, Benjamin W. |
| 19 | Hughes, Charles Evans |
| Diaries | Ickes, Harold L. |
| 1-2 | Ives, Frederic and Herbert |
| B8 | Kingsbury, John A. |
| 4 | Loeb, Jacques |
| 19 | *Morgenthau, Hans J. |
| 8 | Morgenthau, Henry Sr. |
| IIA27 | *NAACP |
| 53 | NAWSA |
| 32, 129 | Oppenheimer, J. Robert |
| | Piccard Family |
| | Reid Family |
| 18 | Russell, Charles Edward |
| 116 | See, Thomas J. |
| | Stone Autograph Collection |
| | Swing, Raymond G. |
| 3 | *Van Doren, Irita B. |
| 4 | Veblen, Oswald |
| 5, 36 | Von Neumann, John |

**EINSTEIN, LEWIS** (1877-1967)  U.S. diplomat, author
1-3  Holmes, Oliver Wendell Jr.
(nearly the entire collection of 300 items consists of correspondence between Holmes and Einstein)

**EIZENSTAT, STUART E.** (1943-  )  U.S. lawyer, government official
3  *Cohen, Benjamin V.

**ELATH, ELIAHU (EPSTEIN)** (1903-  )  Israeli statesman, sociologist
23  Celler, Emanuel
3, 12  *Cohen, Benjamin V.
6  Fahy, Charles
11  *Henderson, Loy W.
9  Mowrer, Edgar A.
14  Meyer, Agnes
  Reid Family

**ERIKSON, ERIK H.** (1902-  )  U.S. psychoanalyst, author, educator
  Lynd, Robert M. and Helen S.
B4, M32, P2  *Mead, Margaret

**ESHKOL, LEVI** (1895-1969)  Israeli statesman, Prime Minister
  Celler, Emanuel
  Reid Family

**FEDERN, PAUL** (1871-1950)  U.S. psychoanalyst
  *Bernfeld, Siegfried
  *Federn, Paul
D18  *Freud, Sigmund
  Weiss, Edoardo

**FEINBERG, CHARLES E.** (1899-  )  U.S. businessman, manuscript collector
  Bacon, Delia S.
6  Clapp, Verner W.
  Feinberg—Karl Shapiro Collection
  Feinberg—Walt Whitman Collection
1  Shapiro, Karl Jay

**FEIS, HERBERT** (1893-1972)  U.S. economist, writer, historian
| | |
|---|---|
| 113 | Cattell, James McKeen |
| 3 | *Cohen, Benjamin V. |
| | *Feis, Herbert |
| 54, 116 | Frankfurter, Felix |
| 12 | Gilchrest, Huntington |
| Diaries | Ickes, Harold L. |
| 33 | Oppenheimer, J. Robert |
| | Schwellenbach, Lewis |
| | Stout, Lesley W. |
| | White, William Allen |

**FERBER, EDNA** (1887-1968)  U.S. author
| | |
|---|---|
| | Ferber, Edna |
| | Gordon, Ruth |
| | Howard, Roy |
| | Kaufman, George S. |
| 8 | Lane, Gertrude |
| | MacLeish, Archibald |
| 7 | Middleton, George |
| | Reid Family |
| 28 | Roosevelt, Theodore, Jr. |
| 1 | Stout, Wesley W. |
| | White, William Allen |

**FEUCHTWANGER, LION** (1884-1958)  German author
| | |
|---|---|
| | Feuchtwanger, Lion |
| | Huebsch, Benjamin W. |

**FLEXNER, ABRAHAM** (1866-1959)  U.S. author, educator
| | |
|---|---|
| B44 | American Council of Learned Societies |
| | *Bollingen Foundation |
| | Bush, Vannevar |
| 10 | *Cairns, Huntington |
| | *Flexner, Abraham |
| 55, 116, 148 | Frankfurter, Felix |
| B9 | Kingsbury, John A. |
| 4 | Loeb, Jacques |

INDIVIDUALS AND CORPORATIONS 37

| | |
|---|---|
| 7 | Middleton, George |
| 34 | Oppenheimer, J. Robert |
| | Reid Family |
| 5, 7, 9 | Rosenwald, Lessing J. |
| | Straus, Oscar S. |
| 5 | Veblen, Oswald |
| 19 | Waterman, Alan J. |
| | Wallace, Henry A. |
| | White, William Allen |

**FLEXNER, BERNARD** (1865-1945)  U.S. lawyer, Zionist leader

| | |
|---|---|
| | Beer, George Louis |
| 3 | *Cohen, Benjamin V. |
| 48 | *Corcoran, Thomas G. |
| | *Flexner, Abraham |
| 55 | Frankfurter, Felix |
| | Lindsey, Ben Barr |

**FORTAS, ABE** (1910-1982)   U.S. Supreme Court Justice, public official, lawyer

| | |
|---|---|
| | American Scholar |
| 59 | *Black, Hugo L. |
| | Celler, Emanuel |
| 3 | *Cohen, Benjamin V. |
| 6 | Fahy, Charles |
| II-5 | Douglas, William O. |
| 135 | Frankfurter, Felix |
| 7-8 | *Graham, Fred |
| II 7 | Ickes, Harold L. |
| | Pinchot, Cornelia |
| 16 | Sobeloff, Simon E. |
| 7 | Straus, Michael Wolf |
| | Wallace, Henry A. |
| 352-53 | Warren, Earl |

## FRANKFURTER, FELIX (1882-1965) U.S. Supreme Court Justice, lawyer, Zionist leader

| | |
|---|---|
| 28, 72 | Ackerman, Carl W. |
| | *Alsop, Joseph and Stewart |
| C256 | American Council of Learned Societies |
| | Baker, Ray Stannard |
| | Beer, George Louis |
| | Berge, Wendell |
| 60 | *Black, Hugo L. |
| 2 | Bowen, Catherine Drinker |
| 7 | Brant, Irving N. |
| 40 | Buck, Solon J. |
| 71, 86, 92, 97, 101, 106 | Burton, Harold H. |
| 110 | Bush, Vannevar |
| 10 | *Cairns, Huntington |
| | Carnegie, Andrew |
| 134 | Clapper, Raymond |
| 8 | *Cohen, Benjamin V. |
| | Commoner, Barry |
| | *Corcoran, Thomas G. |
| | Corcoran, William W. |
| | *Davies, Joseph E. |
| | Douglas, William O. |
| | Edgerton, Henry W. |
| 6 | Fahy, Charles |
| | Farley, James A. |
| 16-7, 32-6 | *Feis, Herbert |
| | Frankfurter, Felix |
| | Frankfurter, Felix—Zionism Collection |
| | Gleason, Arthur H. |
| 1 | Gordon, Ruth |
| 2 | Harrison, Gilbert A. |
| 3 | *Holmes, John Haynes |
| 9 | Huebsch, Benjamin H. |
| Diaries, 57 | Ickes, Harold L. |
| 3, 11 | *Jackson, Robert |

## INDIVIDUALS AND CORPORATIONS

| | |
|---|---|
| 7 | *Jessup, Philip C. |
| | Johnston, Mercer C. |
| 15 | Kanin, Garson |
| B10 | Kingsbury, John A. |
| | Knox, Franklin |
| B97, D12, D17 | *La Follette Family |
| 5 | Landis, James |
| | Leland, Waldo G. |
| | McCoy, Frank R. |
| 7, 45 | MacLeish, Archibald |
| 22 | Meyer, Eugene |
| 7 | Middleton, George |
| | *Morgenthau, Hans J. |
| IC64 | *NAACP |
| | National Woman's Party |
| 6, 24-5 | *Niebuhr, Reinhold |
| 21, 34 | Oppenheimer, J. Robert |
| 10 | *Patterson, Robert P. |
| | Reid Family |
| | Richberg, Donald J. |
| | Roosevelt, Theodore |
| 28 | Roosevelt, Theodore, Jr. |
| 4, 6 | Rosenwald, Lessing J. |
| | Sacco-Vanzetti Case |
| 12 | Sobeloff, Simon |
| 14 | Stephens, Harold |
| 13, 74-5 | Stone, Harlan Fiske |
| | Straus, Oscar S. |
| | Taft, William Howard |
| 4 | *Van Doren, Irita |
| | Warren, Charles |
| 353-4, 663, 756 | Warren, Earl |
| 16 | Wayman, Dorothy G. |
| C51, 56, 66, 75, 82, 120, 137, 203, 215, 246, 267, 286, 317, 342, 375, 414 | White, William Allen |
| | Wilson, Woodrow |

**FREUD, ANNA** (1895-1982) British psychoanalyst
\*Brill, Abraham
\*Freud, Anna
C14 \*Mead, Margaret

**FREUD, SIGMUND** (1856-1939) Austrian psychiatrist, psychoanalyst
Abraham, Karl
Adler, Alfred
1 \*Bernays, Edward L.
1, 14-21 \*Bernfeld, Siegfried
158 \*Bollingen Foundation
1-5 \*Bonaparte, Marie
2-3, 9 \*Brill, Abraham
Einstein, Albert
11 \*Federn, Paul
\*Freud, Anna
\*Freud, Harry
\*Freud, Sigmund
Diaries Ickes, Harold L.
Jelliffe, Smith Ely
4 Loeb, Jacques
2 Lorand, Sandor
3 Weiss, Edoardo

**GINSBERG, ALLEN** (1926- ) U.S. Poet
1 \*Podhoretz, Norman

**GINSBURG, RUTH BADER** (1933- ) U.S. lawyer, educator
128 ERAmerica

**GOLDBERG, ARTHUR J.** (1908- ) U.S. Supreme Court Justice, public official, lawyer
60 \*Black, Hugo L.
7 Brant, Irving N.
13 Brotherhood of Sleeping Car Porters
344 Celler, Emanuel
3 \*Cohen, Benjamin V.

| | | |
|---|---|---|
| II-7 | *Douglas, William O. | |
| 7 | Fahy, Charles | |
| 2 | Harrison, Gilbert A. | |
| | Kroll, Jack | |
| C111 | *Mead, Margaret | |
| 17 | Meyer, Agnes | |
| 29 | Mies van der Rohe, Ludwig | |
| | National Woman's Party | |
| 34 | Owings, Nathaniel | |
| 16 | Sobeloff, Simon E. | |
| 48, 297 | Taft, Charles P. | |
| 354-55 | Warren, Earl | |

**GOLDBERG, RUBE** (1883-1970)  U.S. cartoonist
Nichols, William I.

**GOLDENWEISER, EMANUEL A.** (1883-1953)  U.S. economist
C265  American Council of Learned Societies
Frey, Joseph P.
Goldenweiser, Emanuel
24  Meyer, Eugene
Wallace, Henry A.

**GOLDMAN, EMMA** (1869-1940)  U.S. anarchist, writer, lecturer
C183  American Council of Learned Societies
43  *Gertz, Elmer
4  *Holmes, John Haynes
10  Huebsch, Benjamin W.
8  Middleton, George
13  NAWSA
24, 26  Pinchot, Amos
12  Sanger, Margaret
3  Vander Poel, Halsted

**GOLDMANN, NACHUM** (1894-1982)   Swiss Zionist leader, publisher
11 *Henderson, Loy W.
Diary Ickes, Harold L.
2 Taylor, Myron

**GOLDMARK, PAULINE** (1873-1962)   U.S. social worker
Goldmark, Pauline
National Consumers League

**GOMPERS, SAMUEL** (1850-1924)   U.S. labor leader
Aldrich, Nelson
B45-6 Allen, Henry J.
American Federation of Labor
Baker, Ray Stannard
Borah, William E.
115 Cattell, James McKeen
Croffut, William A.
Foulke, William D.
Frey, Joseph P.
59 Frankfurter, Felix
17 Lansing, Robert
B63, 84, 89 *La Follette Family
75 Murdock, Victor
National Women's Trade Union League of America
Olney, Richard
Redfield Family
Reid Family
Roosevelt, Theodore
28 Roosevelt, Theodore, Jr.
Shields, J. V. A.
Straus, Oscar S.
32 Sweetser, Arthur
Tumulty, Joseph P.
55 Washington, Booker T.
White, William Allen
Wilson, Woodrow

INDIVIDUALS AND CORPORATIONS 43

**GRATZ, BENJAMIN** (1791-1883)     U.S. merchant, philanthropist
           Blair Family
           Gratz, Benjamin
           Mordecai, Alfred

**GRATZ, REBECCA** (1781-1869)     U.S. philanthropist
           Gratz, Rebecca
           Mordecai, Alfred

**GRUENBERG, SIDONIE M.** (1881-1974)     U.S. child specialist, writer, educator
           Gruenberg, Benjamin C. and Sidonie M.
C24-26, 28, 30     *Mead, Margaret

**HECHT, ANTHONY** (1923- )     U.S. poet
1     *Podhoretz, Norman

**HECHT, BEN** (1894- )     U.S. dramatist, playwright
           Hecht, Ben
9     MacLeish, Archibald
           Wallace, Henry A.

**HEIFETZ, JASCHA** (1901- )     U.S. violinist
184     *Bernays, Edward L.
2     Meier, Nellie Simmons

**HEINE, HEINRICH** (1797-1856)     German poet and essayist
81     *Moore, Merrill

**HELLMAN, LILLIAN** (1905-1984)     U.S. dramatist
10     *Arendt, Hannah
3     Flanner-Solano
2     Harrison, Gilbert A.
           Hellman, Lillian
13     Huebsch, Benjamin W.
9     MacLeish, Archibald
9     Middleton, George

| | |
|---|---|
| 1 | *Podhoretz, Norman |
| 12 | Sanger, Margaret |

**HERTZBERG ARTHUR** (1921-    )    U.S. rabbi, author, Zionist leader
| | |
|---|---|
| 1 | *Podhoretz, Norman |

**HERZL, THEODOR** (1860-1904)   Austrian journalist, founder of political Zionism
| | |
|---|---|
| L41 | Celler, Emanuel |
| | National Civic Federation |

**HILLMAN, SIDNEY** (1887-1946)                      U.S. labor leader
| | |
|---|---|
| 67 | Frankfurter, Felix |
| | Frey, Joseph P. |
| Diaries | Ickes, Harold L. |
| | Kroll, Jack |
| D17 | *La Follette Family |
| 9 | MacLeish, Archibald |
| | National Woman's Party |
| | NWTUL |
| | Reid Family |
| | Wallace, Henry A. |

**HIRSCH, MAURICE DE** (1831-1896)         German businessman, philanthropist
| | |
|---|---|
| | Straus, Oscar S. |

**HIRSCHMANN, IRA A.** (1906-1980)   U.S. business executive, diplomat
| | |
|---|---|
| | *Corcoran, Thomas G. |
| 60 | Frankfurter, Felix |
| 10 | MacLeish, Archibald |
| 2 | Malina, Frank J. |
| 27 | Meyer, Eugene |
| 44-5 | Steinhardt, Laurence A. |
| | Wallace, Henry A. |

INDIVIDUALS AND CORPORATIONS 45

**HOUDINI, HARRY** (1874-1926)            U.S. magician
19          Batchelder, John D.
           Kellock, Katherine A.
154        Roosevelt, Kermit
5           *Van Doren, Irita B.

**HOWE, IRVING** (1920-  )         U.S. writer, critic, educator
10          *Arendt, Hannah
           *Bollingen Foundation
2           Harrison, Gilbert A.

**HUEBSCH, BENJAMIN W.** (1876-1964)       U.S. publisher
           Ford Peace Plan
           *Holmes, John H.
           Huebsch, Benjamin W.
           *La Follette Family
           Traubel, Horace

**HURST, FANNIE** (1889-1968)           U.S. author
           Howard, Roy
           Huebsch, Benjamin, W.
           Maxwell, Perriton
9           Middleton, George
           Morgenthau, Henry Sr.
           Roosevelt, Kermit
           Russell, Charles Edward
85         Sanger, Margaret

**JAVITS, JACOB K.** (1904-1986)     U.S. Congressman, Senator, lawyer
8           Brant, Irving N.
15          Brotherhood of Sleeping Car Porters
16          *Cairns, Huntington
4           *Cohen, Benjamin V.
19          Granik, Samuel T.
           Halsey, William F.
           Klein, Julius
14          Mowrer, Edgar A.
           National Woman's Party

46	The Jewish Experience

| | |
|---|---|
| 7 | *Niebuhr, Reinhold |
| 38 | Overholser, Winfred |
| | *Patterson, Robert P. |
| | Reid Family |
| 155 | Roosevelt, Kermit |
| 233 | Spivak, Lawrence E. |
| 53 | Taft, Charles P. |

**KAUFMAN, GEORGE S.** (1889-1961)　　　　U.S. playwright
　　　　　　　　*Alsop, Joseph and Stewart
1　　　　　　　Gordon, Ruth
　　　　　　　　Kaufman, George S.
　　　　　　　　Middleton, George

**KISSINGER, HENRY A.** (1923-　)　　U.S. Secretary of State, educator, historian
　　　　　　　　*Arendt, Hannah
　　　　　　　　*Commoner, Barry
　　　　　　　　*Kissinger, Henry A.
　　　　　　　　*Luce, Henry R.
12　　　　　　　MacLeish, Archibald
　　　　　　　　Mathews, F. David
C86　　　　　　*Mead, Margaret
　　　　　　　　*Morgenthau, Hans J.
15　　　　　　　Mowrer, Edgar A.
43　　　　　　　Oppenheimer, J. Robert
9　　　　　　　*Podhoretz, Norman
238, 240, 242　Spivak, Lawrence E.

**KLEIN, JULIUS** (1901-　)　　U.S. Army officer, journalist, publisher
69　　　　　　　Bristol, Mark L.
14　　　　　　　Halsey, William F.
　　　　　　　　Klein, Julius
　　　　　　　　*Patterson, Robert P.
　　　　　　　　Reid Family
61　　　　　　　Roosevelt, Kermit

34, 422, 455, 907,        *Taft, Robert A.
989, 1127-28, 1234
51                        *Vandenberg, Hoyt S.

**KOCH, EDWARD I.** (1924-      )      U.S. Congressman, mayor, attorney
9                         *Podhoretz, Norman

**KOLLECK, TEDDY** (1911-      ) Israeli public official, Mayor of Jerusalem
                          Celler, Emanuel
4                         *Cohen, Benjamin V.
                          Reid Family

**KORDA, ALEXANDER** (1893-1956)     U.S. motion picture producer and
                                                                director
10                        Middleton, George
                          Watterston, Henry

**KRISTOL, IRVING** (1920-     )        U.S. author, editor, educator
10                        *Arendt, Hannah
34                        *Morgenthau, Hans J.
1                         *Podhoretz, Norman

**LASKI, HAROLD J.** (1893-1950)     British political scientist, educator,
                                                                author
39                        *Black, Hugo L.
40                        Buck, Solon J.
17                        *Cairns, Huntington
                          *Corcoran, Thomas G.
II-10                     *Douglas, William O.
20                        *Feis, Herbert
74-5, 98, 145, 151        Frankfurter, Felix
                          Frankfurter, Zionism Collection
                          Gleason, Arthur H.
16                        Huebsch, Benjamin W.
Diaries                   Ickes, Harold L.
                          *La Follette Family
                          Laski, Harold J.

| | |
|---|---|
| 11 | MacLeish, Archibald |
| 32 | Meyer, Eugene |
| | National Woman's Party |
| | Pinchot, Amos |
| | Roosevelt, Theodore |
| 19 | Stone, Harlan Fiske |
| 5 | *Van Doren, Irita B. |
| | Wallace, Henry A. |
| 33 | Willcox, Walter F. |

**LAZARUS, EMMA** (1849-1887)   U.S. poet and essayist
Cleveland, Grover (see Gilder, Helene de Kay to Mrs. Cleveland—11/19, 21/1887)

| | |
|---|---|
| 26 | Wister, Owen |

**LEHMAN, HERBERT H.** (1878-1963)  U.S. banker, Governor of New York

| | |
|---|---|
| 75 | Beard, Daniel Carter |
| 17 | Brotherhood of Sleeping Car Porters |
| 40 | Buck, Solon J. |
| | Children's Crusade for Children |
| | *Corcoran, Thomas, G. |
| | *Flexner, Abraham |
| 75 | Frankfurter, Felix |
| 28 | Furman, Bess |
| 3 | *Holmes, John Haynes |
| 16 | Huebsch, Benjamin H. |
| 71, Diaries | Ickes, Harold L. |
| B13 | Kingsbury, John A. |
| 10 | Lawrie, Lee |
| | Lehman, Herbert H. |
| 33 | Meyer, Eugene |
| 55 | Moral Re-Armament |
| | National Woman's Party |
| 8 | *Niebuhr, Reinhold |
| 45 | Oppenheimer, J. Robert |
| | *Patterson, Robert P. |
| 32 | *Patton, George S. |

INDIVIDUALS AND CORPORATIONS 49

|   | Reid Family |   |
|---|---|---|
| 2 | Rosenwald, Lessing J. |   |
| 5 | Sayre, Francis B. |   |

**LEINSDORF, ERICH** (1912-    )  U.S. conductor, musician
| 220 | *Bernays, Edward L. |
| 11  | MacLeish, Archibald |
|     | Wallace, Henry A. |

**LEVENTHAL, HAROLD** (1915-1979)  U.S. jurist
| 4 | *Cohen, Benjamin V. |
|   | *Leventhal, Harold |

**LEVI, EDWARD H.** (1911-    )  U.S. public official, lawyer, educator
| 43   | Celler, Emanuel |
| II-10 | Douglas, William O. |
| 9    | Fahy, Charles |
|      | *Morgenthau, Hans J. |

**LEVY, JEFFERSON M.** (1852-1924)  U.S. public official, attorney
|  | Cleveland, Grover |
| Vol. 3, | Trenholm, William L. |
| f. 412 |  |

**LEWIS, JERRY** (1926-    )  U.S. comedian, producer, director
|  | Marx, Groucho |

**LEWISOHN, LUDWIG** (1882-1955)  U.S. novelist and essayist
| C270 | American Council of Learned Societies |
| 17   | Huebsch, Benjamin W. |
|      | Gleason, Arthur H. |
| 6    | *Van Doren, Irita B. |

**LILIENTHAL, DAVID E.** (1899-1981)  U.S. public official, lawyer
|    | Beyer, Otto S. |
| 65 | Bush, Vannevar |
| 1  | Chase, Stuart |

| | |
|---|---|
| 9 | Fahy, Charles |
| 77, 193 | Frankfurter, Felix |
| | Frey, Joseph P. |
| Diaries | Ickes, Harold L. |
| | King, Judson |
| | Krug, Julius A. |
| E7 | *La Follette Family |
| 6, 24 | Landis, James M. |
| 12 | MacLeish, Archibald |
| | Middleton, George |
| 11 | Milton, George F. |
| 16 | Mowrer, Edgar and Lillian |
| 62 | Nichols, William I. |
| 46 | Oppenheimer, J. Robert |
| | Oxnam, G. Bromley |
| | Parsons, William S. |
| | *Patterson, Robert P. |
| 18 | Pulitzer, Joseph II |
| | Reid Family |
| | Richberg, Donald R. |
| 9 | Rosenwald, Lessing J. |
| 6 | *Van Doren, Irita B. |
| | Wallace, Henry A. |
| | White, William Allen |

**LILIENTHAL, OTTO** (1848-1896)                German inventor, aeronaut
| | |
|---|---|
| 63 | American Institute of Aeronautics and Astronautics |
| 9 | Chanute, Octave |

**LINOWITZ, SOL M.** (1913-     ) U.S. public official, corporate executive, lawyer
| | |
|---|---|
| 4 | *Cohen, Benjamin V. |
| 16 | Mowrer, Edgar and Lillian |

**LIPPMAN, WALTER** (1889-1974)                U.S. journalist, author
| | |
|---|---|
| | *Alsop, Joseph and Stewart |
| | American Scholar |

## INDIVIDUALS AND CORPORATIONS

|  |  |
|---|---|
|  | Baker, Newton D. |
| 115 | Baker, Ray Stannard |
| 1 | Balderston, John L. |
| 15 | Biddle, George |
| 4, 33 | Cain, James M. |
| 18 | *Cairns, Huntington |
|  | *Corcoran, Thomas G. |
| 35 | Davis, Norman I. |
| 3, 6 | Eliot, George F. |
| 77-8, 139, 161, 163 | Frankfurter, Felix |
|  | Frankfurter Zionism Collection |
| 3 | Hackworth, Green H. |
| 26 | Ghent, William J. |
| 15 | Gilchrest, Huntington |
|  | Gleason, Arthur H. |
| 8 | Harrison, Gilbert A. |
| 17 | Huebsch, Benjamin W. |
| Diaries | Ickes, Harold L. |
|  | Kellogg, Frank B. |
| 13 | King, Ernest J. |
| A37 | Kingsbury, John A. |
|  | Knox, Franklin |
| B64 | *La Follette Family |
|  | Lindsey, Benjamin Barr |
| 12, 48 | MacLeish, Archibald |
| 56 | *Malik, Charles H. |
| 22 | Marshall, Charles C. |
| C3 | *Mead, Margaret |
|  | Meyer, Agnes |
| 130 | Meyer, Eugene |
| 11 | Middleton, George |
| 63 | Moore, Merrill |
|  | *Morganthau, Hans J. |
| 16 | Mowrer, Edgar and Lillian |
| 47 | Oppenheimer, J. Robert |
|  | Osborn, Fairfield |

| | | |
|---|---|---|
| 13 | *Patterson, Robert P. | |
| 100 | Pinchot, Amos | |
| 18 | Pulitzer, Joseph II | |
| | Reid Family | |
| 64, 155 | Roosevelt, Kermit | |
| | Roosevelt, Theodore | |
| 29 | Roosevelt, Theodore, Jr. | |
| 33 | Sweetser, Arthur | |
| | Taft, William Howard | |
| 67 | Tumulty, Joseph P. | |
| 6 | *Van Doren, Irita B. | |
| | Washburn, Stanley | |
| | White, William Allen | |
| | Wilson, Woodrow | |

**LIPSET, SEYMOUR M.** (1922-    )                    U.S. sociologist
1              Lynd, Robert S. and Helen M.

**LIPSKY, LOUIS** (1876-1973)              U.S. editor, Zionist leader
4              Morgenthau, Henry Sr.
               Straus, Oscar S.
               Roosevelt, Theodore
               Wilson, Woodrow

**LOEB, JACQUES** (1859-1924)           U.S. physiologist, educator
               Arrhenius, Svante August
               Loeb, Jacques

**LOWENTHAL, MAX** (      -1971)    U.S. lawyer, government official
               *Cohen, Benjamin, V.
               *Corcoran, Thomas G.
79             Frankfurter, Felix

**LUDWIG, EMIL** (1881-1948)              Swiss historian and writer
               Huebsch, Benjamin W.
               Ludwig, Emil

**MACK, JULIAN** (1866-1943)     U.S. jurist, communal activist, Zionist leader

|  |  |
|---|---|
|  | Beer, George Louis |
| 2 | *Bernfeld, Siegfried |
| 4 | *Cohen, Benjamin V. |
|  | *Corcoran, Thomas G. |
| 81, 117 | Frankfurter, Felix |
|  | Frankfurter Zionism Collection |
|  | Gleason, Arthur H. |
| Diaries | Ickes, Harold L. |
| 14 | Lansing, Robert |
|  | Lindsey, Benjamin Barr |
|  | Nielson, Fred K. |
| 13 | *Patterson, Robert P. |
|  | Straus, Oscar S. |
|  | Taft, William Howard |
|  | Wilson, Woodrow |

**MAGNES, JUDAH L.** (1877-1948)   U.S. and Israeli religious, educational, and Zionist leader

|  |  |
|---|---|
| 11 | *Arendt, Hannah |
| 304 | Carnegie, Andrew |
| 51 | Celler, Emanuel |
| 28 | Frankfurter, Felix |
| 4 | *Holmes, John Haynes |
| 18 | Huebsch, Benjamin W. |
|  | Loeb, Jacques |
| 46 | Meyer, Eugene |
| 4, 5, 8 | Rosenwald, Lessing J. |
| 9 | Straus, Oscar S. |
|  | Taft, William Howard |
|  | Wilson, Woodrow |

**MAILER, NORMAN** (1923-    )                    U.S. author

|  |  |
|---|---|
| C127 | *Mead, Margaret |
| 6 | *Podhoretz, Norman |
| 1 | Shapiro, Karl Jay |

**MALAMUD, BERNARD** (1914-1986) U.S. writer
9           Jackson, Shirley
13          MacLeish, Archibald
1           Shapiro, Karl Jay

**MARCUS, JACOB R.** (1896-    )    U.S. author, educator, historian
18          *Arendt, Hannah
4           *Cohen, Benjamin V.
8           Doysie, Abel

**MARSHALL, LOUIS** (1856-1929)    U.S. Jewish communal and Zionist
                                                    leader, lawyer
            Baker, Newton D.
            Borah, William E.
            Celler, Emanuel
            Coolidge, Calvin
            Frankfurter, Felix
            Hughes, Charles Evans
4           Lansing, Robert
            Morgenthau, Henry Sr.
            National Civic Federation
            Roosevelt, Theodore
            Stone, Harlan Fiske
            Straus, Oscar S.
            Taft, William Howard

**MARX, HARPO** (1893-1964)                     U.S. comedian
4           Gordon, Ruth
29          Roosevelt, Theodore Jr.

**MARX, KARL** (1818-1883)    German philosopher, writer, founder of
                                                      Communism
41          *Arendt, Hannah
            Marx, Karl

**MEIR, GOLDA** (1898-1978)    Israeli public official, Prime Minister
23          Celler, Emanuel
5           *Garment, Leonard

INDIVIDUALS AND CORPORATIONS 55

                *Kissinger, Henry A.
                Reid Family
246          Spivak, Lawrence E.

**MEYER, EUGENE** (1875-1959)          U.S. news executive
                Bingham, Robert W.
19            Brotherhood of Sleeping Car Porters
84            Frankfurter, Felix
Diaries       Ickes, Harold L.
                *Mills, Ogden L.
                Montgomery Family
61            Moral Re-Armament
                Meyer, Eugene
18            Mowrer, Edgar and Lillian
20            Pulitzer, Joseph II
                Reid Family
                Terrell, Mary Church
                Wallace, Henry A.

**MIKVA, ABNER J.** (1926- )     U.S. attorney, jurist, public official
40            *Morgenthau, Hans J.

**MILLER, ARTHUR** (1915- )              U.S. dramatist
41            Celler, Emanuel
                *Michener, James
1             Shapiro, Karl Jay

**MORDECAI, ALFRED** (1804-1887)     U.S. army officer, engineer
                Jackson, Andrew
                Mordecai, Alfred
                Osborn, Fairfield
                Wheelock, John H.

**MORGENTHAU, HANS J.** (1904-1980)   U.S. political scientist, educator,
                                                      author
82            *Alsop, Joseph and Stewart
                *Arendt, Hannah
                Bingham, June

| | |
|---|---|
| 4 | *Cohen, Benjamin V. |
| 2 | *Corcoran, Thomas G. |
| | Dreikurs, Rudolf |
| | *Kissinger, Henry A. |
| | *Niebuhr, Reinhold |
| | Oppenheimer, J. Robert |
| | Spivak, Lawrence E. |

**MORGENTHAU, HENRY JR.** (1891-1967)   U.S. public official, Zionist leader

| | |
|---|---|
| | *Alsop, Joseph and Stewart |
| 280 | Arnold, Henry H. |
| 18 | Bingham, Robert W. |
| 40 | Buck, Solon J. |
| 25 | *Cairns, Huntington |
| 4 | *Cohen, Benjamin V. |
| | *Corcoran, Thomas G. |
| 91 | Daniels, Josephus |
| | *Davies, Joseph E. |
| II-III | *Douglas, William O. |
| 53 | French, Daniel Chester |
| 85 | Frankfurter, Felix |
| 15 | Halsey, William F. |
| 12 | *Henderson, Loy W. |
| Diaries | Ickes, Harold L. |
| | Johnson, Nelson T. |
| 13 | King, Ernest J. |
| A33, B15 | Kingsbury, John A. |
| 25 | Landis, James M. |
| | Long, Breckinridge |
| 7 | McLean, Evalyn Walsh |
| 14 | MacLeish, Archibald |
| 36 | Meyer, Eugene |
| | Morgenthau, Henry Sr. |
| 84 | Murdock, Victor |
| 21, 42 | *Patterson, Robert P. |

|  |  |
|---|---|
|  | Pittman, Key |
|  | Reid Family |
| 71 | Roosevelt, Kermit |
| 6 | Rosenwald, Lessing J. |
| 1 | Schwellenbach, Lewis |
| 22 | Stone, Harlan Fiske |
| 39 | Sweetser, Arthur |
| 60 | Taft, Charles P. |
| 2 | Taylor, Myron |
|  | White, William Allen |
|  | Williams, Charl Ormond |

**MORGENTHAU, HENRY SR.** (1856-1946)   U.S. statesman, businessman

|  |  |
|---|---|
| 31 | Ackerman, Carl W. |
| 91, 116 | Baker, Ray Stannard |
|  | Bingham, Robert W. |
| 91 | Daniels, Josephus |
| 85 | Frankfurter, Felix |
| Diaries | Ickes, Harold L. |
| B15 | Kingsbury, John A. |
| 52 | Lansing, Robert |
|  | Lindsey, Benjamin Barr |
| 40 | *Morgenthau, Hans J. |
|  | Morgenthau, Henry Sr. |
|  | National Civic Federation |
|  | Reid Family |
| 71 | Roosevelt, Kermit |
|  | Roosevelt, Theodore |
| 95 | Sanger, Margaret |
|  | Straus, Oscar S. |
|  | Taft, William Howard |
| 23 | Watterson, Henry |
| 27 | Wilson, Edith Bolling |
|  | Wilson, Woodrow |
| 14 | Woolley, Robert W. |

**MOSES, ROBERT** (1888-1981)  U.S. public official, author
85                Frankfurter, Felix
43                Nichols, William I.
18                Ogilvy, David
43                *Patterson, Robert P.
                  Reid Family
71                Roosevelt, Kermit
60                Taft, Charles P.
                  White, William Allen

**MUNI, PAUL** (1895-1967)  U.S. actor
13                Middleton, George

**NEUMANN, EMANUEL** (1893-    )  U.S. Zionist leader, attorney
23                Celler, Emanuel
5                 Rosenwald, Lessing J.

**NIZER, LOUIS** (1902-    )  U.S. lawyer, author
20                Mowrer, Edgar A.
                  Nizer, Louis
                  *Patterson, Robert P.
D91               Reid Family
                  Wallace, Henry A.

**NOAH, MORDECAI MANUEL** (1785-1851)  U.S. editor, politician, playwright
513               Adams Family
                  Biddle, Nicholas
                  Curry, Jabez L. M.
                  Fish, Hamilton
                  Green, Duff
                  Jefferson, Thomas
                  Madison, James
                  Marcy, William
                  Monroe, James
                  Schoolcraft, Henry Rowe
                  Tyler, John
                  Van Buren, Martin

## OCHS, ADOLPH S. (1858-1935)   U.S. publisher
        Bingham, Robert Worth
        Bristol, Mark L.
        Howard, Roy
        McKinley, William
        Pulitzer, Joseph II
        Reid Family
        Roosevelt, Theodore
        Schurz, Carl
        Straus, Oscar S.
        Taft, William Howard
        Wilson, Woodrow

## ODETS, CLIFFORD (1906-1963)   U.S. dramatist
5       Krutch, Joseph W.
14      Middleton, George
        Odets, Clifford

## OPPENHEIMER, J. ROBERT (1904-1967)   U.S. public official, scientist, physician
4       Anderson, Clinton P.
89      Bush, Vannevar
47      Celler, Emanuel
        Commoner, Barry
22      *Feis, Herbert
87      Frankfurter, Felix
17      MacLeish, Archibald
        *Morgenthau, Hans J.
        Oppenheimer, J. Robert
        Reid Family
48      Rosenwald, Lessing J.
9       Veblen, Oswald
11      Von Neumann, John
32      Waterman, Alan T.

## PARKER, DOROTHY (1893-1967)   U.S. poet and author
15      MacLeish, Archibald
        Reid Family

| | | |
|---|---|---|
| 1 | Stout, Wesley W. | |
| | Wallace, Henry A. | |

**PERLMUTTER, NATHAN** (1923-    )     U.S. executive director
1          *Podhoretz, Norman

**PERELMAN, S. J.** (1904-1979)           U.S. writer, humorist
           Davis, Elmer
           Flanner-Solano
3          Harrison, Gilbert A.
           Marx, Groucho

**PERES, SHIMON** (1923-    )    Israeli soldier, Prime Minister, public official
           *Kissinger, Henry A.
244        Spivak, Lawrence E.

**POOL, DAVID DE SOLA** (1885-1970)     U.S. religious, civic, and communal leader, historian
36         Celler, Emanuel
C15, 19    *Mead, Margaret

**PULITZER, JOSEPH** (1847-1911)       U.S. journalist, publisher
           Pulitzer, Joseph (1847-1911)
           Pulitzer, Joseph (1885-1955)

**RABI, ISIDORE I.** (1898-    )           U.S. physicist
95         Bush, Vannevar
59         Oppenheimer, J. Robert

**RABIN, YITZCHAK** (1922-    )    Israeli soldier, public official, Prime Minister
5          *Garment, Leonard
           *Kissinger, Henry

**RAYNER, ISIDORE** (1850-1912)       U.S. Senator and lawyer
           Roosevelt, Theodore
           Straus, Oscar S.

INDIVIDUALS AND CORPORATIONS 61

                Taft, William Howard
                Wilson, Woodrow

**RIBICOFF, ABRAHAM A.** (1910- )    U.S. Senator, public official
24              Brotherhood of Sleeping Car Porters
12              Chase, Stuart
50              Furman, Bess
3               Harrison, Gilbert A.
38              Mearns, David A.
24, 112         Mowrer, Edgar and Lillian
                National Woman's Party
                *Ribicoff, Abraham A.
                Spivak, Lawrence E.

**RICKOVER, HYMAN G.** (1900- )    U. S. naval officer, government official
                Commoner, Barry
45              Nichols, William I.

**ROBINSON, EDWARD G.** (1893-1973)    U.S. actor
                *Cain, James M.
15              Middleton, George

**ROSE, ERNESTINE L.S.P.** (1810-1892)    U.S. feminist, reformer
73              NAWSA

**ROSENBERG, ETHEL AND JULIUS** (1920-1953/1918-1953)    Convicted U.S. spies
C295            American Council of Learned Societies
84, 125         *McGranery, James P.
62              Oppenheimer, J. Robert
                Rogge, Oetje John

**ROSENMAN, SAMUEL I.** (1896-1973)    U.S. lawyer, jurist, Presidential advisor
23              *Corcoran, Thomas
                *Davies, Joseph E.
13              Fahy, Charles

|  |  |
|---|---|
| 99 | Frankfurter, Felix |
|  | Ickes, Harold L. |
| 19 | MacLeish, Archibald |
|  | *Patterson, Robert P. |

**ROSENWALD, LESSING JULIUS** (1891-1979)　　U.S. businessman, philanthropist, art collector

|  |  |
|---|---|
|  | Borglum, John Gutzon |
| 146 | Cattell, James McKeen |
|  | Fisher, Walter L. |
|  | Flexner, Abraham |
|  | Ford Peace Plan |
| 12 | *Henderson, Loy W. |
| 11 | Lansing, Robert |
| 19 | MacLeish, Archibald |
| C64 | *Mead, Margaret |
| 40 | Meyer, Eugene |
|  | Reid Family |
| Ethnic and Racial Groups— Jews (German) | United States Works Progress Administration |
|  | Washington, Booker T. |
|  | White, William Allen |
|  | Woodson, Carter G. |

**ROSTEN, LEO C.** (1908-　)　　U.S. author, political scientist

|  |  |
|---|---|
|  | Ickes, Harold L. |
| 19 | MacLeish, Archibald |
| 50 | *Morgenthau, Hans J. |

**ROTH, PHILIP** (1933-　)　　U.S. author

|  |  |
|---|---|
| 3 | Harrison, Gilbert A. |
| 6 | *Podhoretz, Norman |
|  | *Roth, Philip |

**RUBY, JACK** (1911-1967)　　U.S., slayer of Lee Harvey Oswald

|  |  |
|---|---|
|  | *Gertz, Elmer |
| 760 | Warren, Earl |

## RUKEYSER, MURIEL (1913-1980) U.S. poet

C21, 25, 75, 78
Ciardi, John
*Mead, Margaret
Rukeyser, Muriel
Wickes, Frances G.

## SALOMON, EDWARD SELIG (1836-1913) U.S. Army officer, Governor of Washington Territory

Garfield, James A.
Grant, Ulysses S. (see Solomon)
Taft, William Howard

## SALOMON, HAYM (1740-1785) U.S. Revolutionary War patriot, merchant

21
Fitzpatrick, John C.
Franklin, Benjamin
Morris, Robert

18, 31, 46
Russell, Charles Edward

## SAPHIRSTEIN, JACOB (1853-1914) U.S. publisher

Roosevelt, Theodore
Taft, William Howard
Wilson, Woodrow

## SARNOFF, DAVID (1891-1971) U.S. businessman, broadcaster

Block, Claude C.

46
*Corcoran, Thomas G.

101
Frankfurter, Felix
Granik, Samuel T.
Hooper, Stanford

12
Lawrie, Lee

25
Mowrer, Edgar and Lillian

62-65
O'Laughlin, John C.
Reid Family
Wallace, Henry A.

**SCHIFF, JACOB** (1847-1920)  U.S. banker, philanthropist, Jewish communal leader

                Cleveland, Grover
                Lansing, Robert
                McAdoo, William G.
                McKinley, William
                Morgenthau, Henry Sr.
A149          Reid Family
                Roosevelt, Theodore
                Straus, Oscar S.
                Taft, William Howard
                Washington, Booker T.
                Wilson, Woodrow

**SCHOLEM, GERSHOM GERHARD** (1897-1982)  Israeli author
12             *Arendt, Hannah
3              *Bernfeld, Siegfried

**SCHWIMMER, ROSIKA** (1877-1948)  Hungarian public official, political activist
22            Blackwell Family
3              Bowen, Catherine D.
8              Catt, Carrie Chapman
                Ford Peace Plan
182           Frankfurter, Felix
25            Huebsch, Benjamin W.
                Lindsey, Benjamin Barr
27, 73       National American Woman Suffrage Association
                National Woman's Party
                Schwimmer, Rosika
                Wilson, Woodrow

**SELTZER, MICHAEL I.** (   -   )  U.S. political scientist
541           *Morgenthau, Hans J.
                Selzer, Michael I.

**SHAHN, BEN** (1898-1969)  U.S. artist
16            Biddle, George

## INDIVIDUALS AND CORPORATIONS

**SHAPIRO, KARL JAY** (1913-    )   U.S. poet, editor, educator
33   *Cairns, Huntington
     Ciardi, John
     Shapiro, Karl Jay
     Tolson, Melvin B.

**SHARET (SHERTOK), MOSHE** (1894-1965)   Israeli government official
23   Celler, Emanuel

**SHAZAR, ZALMAN,** (1889-1974)   Israeli statesman, President
2    *Cohen, Benjamin V.
1    *Podhoretz, Norman

**SILVER, ABBA HILLEL** (1893-1963)   U.S. religious and Zionist leader
23       Celler, Emanuel
102      Frankfurter, Felix
12       *Henderson, Loy W.
Diaries  Ickes, Harold L.
648      Taft, Robert A.
         Wallace, Henry A.

**SINGER, ISAAC BASHEVIS** (1904-    )   U.S. author, journalist
4    Shapiro, Karl Jay

**SOBELOFF, SIMON E.** (1893-1973)   U.S. lawyer, public official
51    *Black, Hugo L.
33    *Cairns, Huntington
14    Fahy, Charles
102   Frankfurter, Felix
      *Jackson, Robert
      Reid Family
      Sobeloff, Simon E.
      Wallace, Henry A.

**SPINGARN, ARTHUR B.** (1878-1971)   U.S. lawyer, author, co-founder of NAACP
26   Brotherhood of Sleeping Car Porters
     *Mills, Ogden

IC74 *NAACP
*Spingarn, Arthur B.

**SPINGARN, JOEL E.** (1875-1939)　　U.S. literary scholar, co-founder of NAACP

C171 American Council of Learned Societies
Bethune, Mary Jane M.
*NAACP
Storey, Moorfield

**SPINOZA, BARUCH** (1632-1677)　　Dutch philosopher
*Einstein, Albert (work of Willy Aron on Spinoza)
811 German Captured Documents (manuscript, in French, by Henri Serouya)

**SPIVAK, LAWRENCE E.** (1900-　)　　U.S. producer, publisher, political analyst

Reid Family
Spivak, Lawrence E.

**STEIN, GERTRUDE** (1874-1946)　　U.S. author
Biddle, George
Davidson, Jo
4, 6 Flanner-Solano
11-12 Harrison, Gilbert A.
16 Middleton, George

**STEINHARDT, LAWRENCE A.** (1892-1950)　　U.S. diplomat, lawyer, economist

32 Ackerman, Carl W.
26 *Feis, Herbert
41 Meyer, Eugene
Reid Family
Steinhardt, Lawrence A.
Wallace, Henry A.

**STERN, ISAAC** (1920-　)　　U.S. violinist
1 *Podhoretz, Norman

INDIVIDUALS AND CORPORATIONS 67

**STONE, ISIDORE FEINSTEIN** (1907-    )  U.S. journalist
  *Corcoran, Thomas G.

**STRAUS, OSCAR S.** (1850-1926)  U.S. Secretary of Commerce, diplomat, businessman

|       |                                    |
|-------|------------------------------------|
|       | Bayard, Thomas F.                  |
|       | Carnegie, Andrew                   |
|       | Carpenter, Frank                   |
| 150   | Cattell, James McKeen              |
|       | Cleveland, Grover                  |
|       | Cortelyou, George B.               |
| 9     | Fuller, Melville W.                |
|       | Gresham, Walter Q.                 |
|       | Harrison, Benjamin                 |
|       | Hughes, Charles Evans              |
| A36   | Kinglsbury, John A.                |
|       | Lansing, Robert L.                 |
|       | Lindsey, Benjamin Barr             |
|       | McKinley, William                  |
| 41    | Meyer, Eugene                      |
| 7, 23 | Moore, John Bassett                |
| 4     | Morgenthau, Henry Sr.              |
|       | National Civic Federation          |
| 67-68 | O'Laughlin, John C.                |
|       | Reid Family                        |
|       | Roosevelt, Theodore                |
|       | Root, Elihu                        |
|       | Schurz, Carl                       |
|       | Straus, Oscar S.                   |
|       | Oscar S. Straus Memorial Association |
|       | Taft, William Howard               |
| C271  | White, William Allen               |
|       | Wilson, James H.                   |
|       | Wilson, Woodrow                    |

**STRAUSS, ROBERT S.** (1918-    )  U.S. lawyer, businessman, public official

| 5       | *Cohen, Benjamin V. |
| 234,241 | Spivak, Lawrence E. |

**SULZBERGER, ARTHUR HAYS** (1891-1968)  U.S. publisher

| | |
|---|---|
| 32 | Ackerman, Carl W. |
| | Baker, Ray Stannard |
| 12 | Biddle, George |
| | Catt, Carrie Chapman |
| 8 | Eaker, Ira C. |
| 106, 160 | Frankfurter, Felix |
| 16 | Halsey, William F. |
| Diaries | Ickes, Harold L. |
| 15 | King, Ernest J. |
| 18 | MacLeish, Archibald |
| 29 | Meyer, Agnes |
| 42 | Meyer, Eugene |
| 16 | Middleton, George |
| 26 | Pulitzer, Joseph II |
| | Reid Family |
| | Roosevelt, Kermit |
| 5, 7 | Rosenwald, Lessing J. |
| 158 | Steinhardt, Lawrence A. |
| 8 | *Van Doren, Irita B. |
| | Wallace, Henry A. |
| | White, William Allen |

**SULZBERGER, MAYER S.** (1843-1923)  U.S. jurist, Jewish communal leader

Straus, Oscar S.
Taft, William Howard
Wilson, Woodrow

**SZILARD, LEO** (1898-1964)  U.S. nuclear and biophysicist

| | |
|---|---|
| | *Morgenthau, Hans J. |
| 70 | Oppenheimer, J. Robert |
| | Physical Review Records |

**SZOLD, HENRIETTA** (1860-1945)  U.S. Zionist leader, health activist

| | |
|---|---|
| 150 | Cattell, James McKeen |
| | Frankfurter Zionism Collection |

| | | |
|---|---|---|
| 75 | National American Woman Suffrage Association | |
| | Straus, Oscar S. | |

**TELLER, EDWARD** (1908-    )        U.S. physicist, author, scientist
6          Gamow, George
C94        *Mead, Margaret
           Murphree, Egar V.
71         Oppenheimer, J. Robert
A1         *Spivak, Lawrence E.
           Teller, Edward
32         Von Neumann, John

**TROTSKY, LEON** (1879-1940)         Russian revolutionary
339        Howard, Roy
77         Pulitzer, Joseph I

**TRILLING, LIONEL** (1905-1975)      U.S. literary critic, educator
1, 12      *Podhoretz, Norman

**TUCHMAN, BARBARA W.** (1912-    )   U.S. author, historian
3          Bowen, Catherine D.
22         MacLeish, Archibald

**UNTERMEYER LOUIS** (1885-1977)      U.S. poet, author, editor
11         Jackson, Shirley
           Kilmer, Alfred Joyce
7          Krutch, Joseph Wood
22         MacLeish, Archibald
           Moore, Merrill
5          Shapiro, Karl J.
           Tewson, William O.
           Untermeyer, Louis
C31, 35, 39, 232,   White, William Allen
399, 417, 429

**URIS, LEON M.** (1924-    )         U.S. author
C34        *Mead, Margaret

**VON NEUMANN, JOHN** (1903-1957) U.S. mathematician
    *Freud, Sigmund
    Oppenheimer, J. Robert
    Veblen, Oswald
    Von Neumann, John
    Wexler, Harry

**WALD, LILLIAN** (1867-1940) U.S. social worker
|   |   |
|---|---|
|    | Baker, Ray Stannard |
| 24 | Blackwell Family |
|    | Dock, Lavinia L. |
| A38 | Kingsbury, John A. |
| B76 | *La Follette Family |
| 17 | Middleton, George |
| 30 | NAWSA |
| 24 | Pinchot, Amos |
|    | Reid Family |
|    | Roosevelt, Theodore |
|    | Taft, William Howard |
| 9 | *Van Doren, Irita B. |
| 246, 281, 386 | Washington, Booker T. |
|    | Wilson, Woodrow |

**WARBURG, FELIX M.** (1871-1937) U.S. banker, philanthropist, communal leader
| | |
|---|---|
| C193 | American Council of Learned Societies |
|    | Coolidge, Calvin |
|    | Frankfurter, Felix |
|    | Morgenthau, Henry M. Sr. |
|    | Reid Family |
|    | Taft, William Howard |

**WEIZMANN, CHAIM** (1874-1952) Israeli President, Zionist leader, chemist
| | |
|---|---|
| 23, 51 | Celler, Emanuel |
|    | Clemens, Cyril |
| 118 | Bush, Vannevar |

INDIVIDUALS AND CORPORATIONS 71

| | |
|---|---|
| 111, 162, 202 | Frankfurter, Felix |
| | Frankfurter Zionism Collection |
| Diaries | Ickes, Harold L. |
| 77, 34 | Oppenheimer, J. Robert |
| | Reid Family |
| | Wilson, Woodrow |

**WEIZMAN, EZER** (1924-    )    Israeli soldier, public official

| | |
|---|---|
| 240 | Spivak, Lawrence E. |

**WISE, STEPHEN S.** (1874-1949)   U.S. religious, communal, and Zionist leader

| | |
|---|---|
| | Baker, Ray Stannard |
| 138 | Beard, Daniel Carter |
| 459 | *Bernays, Edward L. |
| 16 | Brant, Irving N. |
| | Breckinridge Family |
| | Carnegie, Andrew |
| 158 | Cattell, James McKeen |
| 23, 51 | Celler, Emanuel |
| 12 | *Cohen, Benjamin V. |
| 43 | Dodd, William E. |
| II-19 | *Douglas, William O. |
| 164 | Frankfurter, Felix |
| | Frankfurter Zionism Collection |
| | Gleason, Arthur H. |
| 12 | *Henderson, Loy W. |
| 5 | Hertz, Emanuel |
| 4 | *Holmes, John Haynes |
| | Howard, Roy |
| 31 | Huebsch, Benjamin W. |
| Diaries | Ickes, Harold L. |
| | Johnston, Mercer C. |
| | Kennan, George |
| A33, B23 | Kingsbury, John A. |
| 212 | Lindsey, Benjamin Barr |
| | Long, Breckinridge |

| | |
|---|---|
| 20 | MacLeish, Archibald |
| 9 | Morgenthau, Henry M. Sr. |
| 29 | Mowrer, Edgar and Lillian |
| 32 | NAWSA |
| IIA22 | *NAACP |
| 13 | Niebuhr, Reinhold |
| 24-26 | Pinchot, Amos |
| 29 | Pulitzer, Joseph II |
| | Reid Family |
| 101 | Roosevelt, Kermit |
| | Roosevelt, Theodore |
| 18, 33 | Russell, Charles Edward |
| 367 | Sobeloff, Simon |
| | Straus, Oscar S. |
| | Taft, William Howard |
| 2 | Taylor, Myron |
| 94, 211, 817, 914, 952 | Washington, Booker T. |
| | White, William Allen |
| | Wilson, Woodrow |

**WOLF, SIMON** (1836-1923)　　　　　　　　　　　U.S. lawyer, author

| | |
|---|---|
| | Cortelyou, George |
| | Cleveland, Grover |
| 70, 75 | Fish, Hamilton |
| 124, folder 11 | Garfield, James R. |
| | Hay, John |
| | McKinley, William |
| | Roosevelt, Theodore |
| | Straus, Oscar S. |
| | Wilson, Woodrow |
| | Wolf, Simon |

**WOUK, HERMAN** (1915-　)　　　　　　　　　　U.S. author

| | |
|---|---|
| 5 | *Cohen, Benjamin V. |
| 28 | *Feis, Herbert |
| 31 | Huebsch, Benjamin W. |
| C16 | Louchheim, Katie S. |
| 17 | Middleton, George |

**YULEE, DAVID LEVY** (1810-1886)  U.S. Senator, business
executive, Confederate official
Cralle, Richard K. (1859 Aug. 8 & Fe 16)
2                Trenholm, William L. (1865 Oct.)
Davis, Jefferson (1855 Mar. 27 & 1853 Mar. 30)

**ZANGWILL, ISRAEL** (1864-1926)  British author, Zionist leader
16               Fiske, Minnie Maddern
3                *Holmes, John Haynes
4, 5             Morgenthau, Henry M. Sr.
48               Moulton, Louise Chandler
80               NAWSA
                 Straus, Oscar S.
                 Roosevelt, Theodore
                 Wilson, Woodrow

**ZOLA, EMILE** (1840-1902)  French novelist
14               Batchelder, John D.
23               Beach, Joseph W.
                 Zola, Emile

**ZWEIG, STEFAN** (1881-1942)  Austrian writer
16               *Freud, Sigmund
31-2, 41         Huebsch, Benjamin W.
17               Middleton, George
                 Zweig, Stefan

# B. CORPORATIONS

## 1. INSTITUTIONS

**AMERICAN JEWISH ARCHIVES**
8 Doysie, Abel
1 Huebsch, Benjamin W.

**AMERICAN JEWISH HISTORICAL SOCIETY**
53 *Jameson, J. Franklin
4, 5 Rosenwald, Lessing J.
 Straus, Oscar S.

**BOARD OF JEWISH EDUCATION (CHICAGO)**
65 *Gertz, Elmer

**HEBREW UNION COLLEGE–JEWISH INSTITUTE OF RELIGION**
4 *Cohen, Benjamin V.
27 Morgenthau, Hans J.
5, 6, 8, 9 Rosenwald, Lessing J.
358 Sobeloff, Simon

**HEBREW UNIVERSITY (JERUSALEM)**
B51 American Council of Learned Societies
3 *Cohen, Benjamin V.
C16 *Louchheim, Katie S.
35 Meyer, Agnes
129-30 Oppenheimer, J. Robert

**HEBREW UNIVERSITY HOSPITAL**
51                    Meyer, Agnes

**INSTITUTE OF JEWISH AFFAIRS**
                      *Meade, Margaret
30                    *Morgenthau, Hans J.

**JEWISH COMMUNITY CENTER**
36                    Meyer, Agnes
129                   Meyer, Eugene

**JEWISH THEOLOGICAL INSTITUTE**
31                    Arendt, Hannah

**JEWISH THEOLOGICAL SEMINARY OF AMERICA**
37                    Bryson, Lyman L.
36                    Meyer, Agnes
93, 133               Oppenheimer, J. Robert
4, 5, 7               Rosenwald, Lessing J.
359                   Sobeloff, Simon

**TECHNION**
145                   Oppenheimer, J. Robert

**TEL AVIV UNIVERSITY**
145                   Oppenheimer, J. Robert

**UNIVERSITY OF HAIFA**
59                    *Morgenthau, Hans J.

**WASHINGTON HEBREW CONGREGATION**
34                    Bryan, William Jennings (11/21/21)

**WEIZMANN INSTITUTE OF SCIENCE**
332                   Celler, Emanuel
108, 152-53           Oppenheimer, J. Robert

**YESHIVA UNIVERSITY**
51, 364          Celler, Emanuel
23               Halsey, William F.
51               Stone, Harlan Fiske

# 2. ORGANIZATIONS

**ACADEMIC COMMITTEE ON SOVIET JEWRY**
14               *Arendt, Hannah

**AMERICAN COUNCIL FOR JUDAISM**
14               *Arendt, Hannah
33               Celler, Emanuel

**AMERICAN EMERGENCY COMMITTEE FOR ZIONIST AFFAIRS**
4                *Cohen, Benjamin V.

**AMERICAN FRIENDS OF HEBREW UNIVERSITY**
33               Celler, Emanuel
53               *Gertz, Elmer
3                *Morgenthau, Hans J.
351             Sobeloff, Simon

**AMERICAN FRIENDS OF THE MIDDLE EAST**
26               *Luce, Henry R.

**AMERICAN ISRAEL CULTURAL FOUNDATION**
26               *Luce, Henry R.

**AMERICAN ISRAEL PUBLIC AFFAIRS COMMITTEE**
333             Celler, Emanuel

**AMERICAN JEWISH ALLIANCE**
1                Huebsch, Benjamin W.

## AMERICAN JEWISH COMMITTEE

| | |
|---|---|
| 14 | *Arendt, Hannah |
| 1 | Atlantic Union Committee |
| 7, 68 | *Bernays, Edward L. |
| 333 | Celler, Emanuel |
| 4 | *Cohen, Benjamin V. |
| 113 | ERAmerica |
| 1 | Huebsch, Benjamin W. |
| | *Meade, Margaret |
| 91 | Meyer, Eugene |
| 3 | *Morgenthau, Hans J. |
| IIA21, 352, 398 IIIB7, 248-49 | *NAACP |
| | National Council of Jewish Women—Washington, D.C. Office |
| 112 | Oppenheimer, J. Robert |
| 1-2 | *Podhoretz, Norman |
| 3 | Rosenwald, Lessing J. |
| 351 | Sobeloff, Simon E. |

## AMERICAN JEWISH CONGRESS

| | |
|---|---|
| 33, 243 | Celler, Emanuel |
| 113 | ERAmerica |
| 8-11 | *Gertz, Elmer |
| | *Mead, Margaret |
| 3 | *Morgenthau, Hans J. |
| IIA21-22, 352 IIIB6-7, 54-55, 250 | *NAACP |
| | National Council of Jewish Women—Washington, D.C. Office |
| D271 | Reid Family |
| 351-52 | Sobeloff, Simon |

## AMERICAN JEWISH JOINT DISTRIBUTION COMMITTEE

| | |
|---|---|
| 91 | Meyer, Eugene |
| 34 | Rosenwald, Lessing J. |

## AMERICAN JEWISH LEAGUE AGAINST COMMUNISM
1                Standley, William H.

## AMERICAN JEWISH TERCENTENARY
33             Celler, Emanuel
1                Shapiro, Karl Jay
352            Sobeloff, Simon E.

## AMERICAN PALESTINE TRADING CORPORATION
34             Celler, Emanuel

## AMERICAN PROFESSORS FOR PEACE IN THE MIDDLE EAST
15             *Arendt, Hannah
4                *Morgenthau, Hans J.

## AMERICAN ZIONIST COUNCIL
353            Sobeloff, Simon

## AMERICAN ZIONIST EMERGENCY COUNCIL
92             Meyer, Eugene (1943-46)

## AMERICAN ZIONIST FEDERATION
                    National Council of Jewish Women—Washington, D.C. Office

## B'NAI B'RITH
                    Commoner Barry
120            ERAmerica
37             Furman, Bess
9                Mearns, David
5                Meyer, Agnes
97             Meyer, Eugene
                    *Morgenthau, Hans J.
IIA190, 216    *NAACP
25             National Council of Jewish Women—Washington, D.C. Office
67             Sanger, Margaret
353            Sobeloff, Simon

## B'NAI B'RITH—ANTI-DEFAMATION LEAGUE
| | |
|---|---|
| 34 | Celler, Emanuel |
| 10, 14 | *Holmes, John Haynes |
| 43 | Ickes, Harold L. |
| IIIB55 | *NAACP |
| | National Council of Jewish Women—Washington, D.C. Office |
| 2, 3 | Rosenwald, Lessing J. |
| 353, 358 | Sobeloff, Simon |

## B'NAI ZION
311        Celler, Emanuel

## COMMISSION ON SOCIAL ACTION OF REFORM JUDAISM
114        ERAmerica

## CONFERENCE ON ADULT JEWISH EDUCATION
12         Bryson, Lyman L.

## CONFERENCE ON JEWISH PHILOSOPHY
16         *Arendt, Hannah

## CONFERENCE ON JEWISH SOCIAL STUDIES
16         *Arendt, Hannah

## CONFERENCE ON THE STATUS OF SOVIET JEWS
16         *Arendt, Hannah
13         *Morgenthau, Hans J.

## DECALOGUE SOCIETY (ORGANIZATION OF JEWISH ATTORNEYS IN CHICAGO)
32         *Gertz, Elmer

## FEDERATION OF JEWISH PHILANTHROPIES
37         *Bernays, Edward L.
1          *Podhoretz, Norman

**HABIMA THEATRE**
183 *Bernays, Edward L.

**HADASSAH**
41, 267 Celler, Emanuel
35 Meyer, Agnes
83 Sanger, Margaret

**HEBREW COMMITTEE OF NATIONAL LIBERATION**
126 Meyer, Eugene
 Wallace, Henry A. (see Bergson, Peter)
Diary Ickes, Harold L.

**HILLEL FOUNDATION**
27 *Morgenthau, Hans J.

**JEWISH AGENCY**
93 Oppenheimer, J. Robert

**JEWISH AGRICULTURAL SOCIETY**
129 Meyer, Eugene

**JEWISH CHAUTAUQUA SOCIETY**
 Taft, William Howard

**JEWISH COMMUNITY COUNCILS**
15 Sobeloff, Simon E.

**JEWISH COMMUNITY COUNCIL OF CHICAGO**
Diary Ickes, Harold L.

**JEWISH CULTURAL RECONSTRUCTION**
17 *Arendt, Hannah

**JEWISH LABOR COMMITTEE**
IIA330 *NAACP

## JEWISH MENTAL HEALTH SOCIETY
202 *Bernays, Edward L.

## JEWISH MINISTERS' ASSOCIATION
Taft, William Howard

## JEWISH NATIONAL FUND
267 Celler Emanuel
Diary Ickes, Harold L.
358 Sobeloff, Simon

## JEWISH NATIONAL WORKERS ALLIANCE OF AMERICA
Diary Ickes, Harold L.

## JEWISH PALESTINE APPEAL
Diary Ickes, Harold L.

## JEWISH PHILANTHROPIES
12 Ogilvy, David

## JEWISH PUBLICATION SOCIETY
14 Huebsch, Benjamin W.
Taft, William Howard
358 Sobeloff, Simon

## JEWISH WAR VETERANS OF THE UNITED STATES
261, 283 Celler, Emanuel
19 Halsey, William F.
IIA194 *NAACP

## JEWISH WELFARE BOARD
24 *Holmes, John Haynes
Wilson, Woodrow

## JEWISH YOUTH MOVEMENT AND SCHOOL REFORM
5-7 *Bernfeld, Siegfried

## JUDAH MAGNES FOUNDATION
18 *Arendt, Hannah

## MAIMONIDES INSTITUTE
350 Celler, Emanuel

## MISCELLANEOUS—JEWISH ORGANIZATIONS
18 *Arendt, Hannah
37, 50, 63, 75, 86, *Holmes, John Haynes
98, 115, 121, 135,
151, 169
45 Meyer, Eugene
93 Oppenheimer, J. Robert
353, 355, 358, 359, Sobeloff, Simon
363, 367

## MIZRACHI ORGANIZATION OF AMERICA
45 Celler, Emanuel

## MIZRACHI WOMEN OF NEW YORK
275 Celler, Emanuel

## NATIONAL CONFERENCE OF CHRISTIANS AND JEWS
168-70 Baker, Newton D.
IIA363 *NAACP

## NATIONAL CONFERENCE ON SOVIET JEWRY
196 National Conference of Jewish Women—
Washington, D.C. Office

## NATIONAL COUNCIL OF JEWISH WOMEN
7 Catt, Carrie Chapman
45, 351 Celler, Emanuel
117, 130 ERAmerica
B18 National Consumers League
National Council of Jewish Women—National Office

INDIVIDUALS AND CORPORATIONS 83

                    National Council of Jewish Women—Washington, D.C. Office
                    National Women's Party
98               Sanger, Margaret

## NATIONAL FEDERATION OF TEMPLE BROTHERHOODS
111             Sanger, Margaret

## NATIONAL FEDERATION OF TEMPLE SISTERHOODS
117, 130       ERAmerica

## NATIONAL JEWISH WOMEN'S ORGANIZATIONS
IIA363          *NAACP
235             Sanger, Margaret

## NATIONAL LADIES AUXILIARY OF JEWISH WAR VETERANS OF THE U.S.A.
130             ERAmerica

## ORT FEDERATIONS
327             Celler, Emanuel

## PALESTINE ENDOWMENT FUND
4                *Cohen, Benjamin V.

## PALESTINE FOUNDATION FUND
28              Granik, Samuel T.

## PRO–PALESTINE FEDERATION OF AMERICA
5                *Holmes, John Haynes

## RABBINICAL ASSEMBLY OF AMERICA
111             Sanger, Margaret

## UNION OF ORTHODOX RABBIS
111             Sanger, Margaret

## UNITED JEWISH APPEAL
| | |
|---|---|
| 49 | Celler, Emanuel |
| 20 | Harriman, Florence J. |
| 64 | *Luce, Henry R. |
| 143 | Meyer, Eugene |
| 106 | Oppenheimer, J. Robert |
| 58 | Rosenwald, Lessing J. |
| 367 | Sobeloff, Simon E. |

## UNITED LUBAVITCHER YESHIVOT
360            Celler, Emanuel

## UNITED SYNAGOGUE OF AMERICA
111            Sanger, Margaret
215            National Conference of Jewish Women—Washington, D.C. Office

## UNKNOWN JEWISH MARTYR
49             Celler, Emanuel

## VAAD HATZALA REHABILITATION COMMITTEE
49             Celler, Emanuel

## WASHINGTON HEBREW CONGREGATION
34             Bryan, William Jennings (11/21/21)
3              *Cohen, Benjamin V.

## WEIZMANN, WORLD MEMORIAL COMMITTEE
152-53         Oppenheimer, J. Robert

## WORLD ZIONIST ORGANIZATION
1              *Podhoretz, Norman

## YOUTH ALIYAH
51             Celler, Emanuel
515            *Luce, Clare Boothe

## ZIONIST ORGANIZATION OF AMERICA
| | |
|---|---|
| 51 | Celler, Emanuel |
| 3 | *Cohen, Benjamin V. |
| 165 | Meyer, Eugene (1934-49) |
| 200-15 | National Council of Jewish Women—Washington, D.C. Office |
| 367 | Sobeloff, Simon |

# 3. PUBLICATIONS

## THE AMERICAN HEBREW
33          Celler, Emanuel

## AMERICAN HEBREW AND JEWISH TRIBUNE
68          *Bernays, Edward L.

## AMERICAN JEWISH CONGRESS DIGEST
14          Sobeloff, Simon E.

## AUFBAU
            *Arendt, Hannah

## CHICAGO JEWISH FORUM
22          *Gertz, Elmer

## COMMENTARY
13          *Morgenthau, Hans J.
2           *Podhoretz, Norman

## CONTEMPORARY JEWISH RECORD
3           Shapiro, Karl Jay (see Rahv, Philip)

## ISRAEL MAGAZINE
19          *Feis, Herbert (1966-67)

**JEWISH CHRONICLE**
302                      Celler, Emanuel

**JEWISH COMMENT**
                         Taft, William Howard

**JEWISH DAILY COURIER**
Diary                    Ickes, Harold L.

**JEWISH DAILY NEWS**
                         Taft, William Howard

**JEWISH LIFE**
IIA-330                  *NAACP

**JEWISH MORNING JOURNAL**
                         Rosenwald, Lessing J.
                         Taft, William Howard

**JEWISH NEWSLETTER**
9                        Rosenwald, Lessing J.

**JEWISH TRIBUNE**
C105                     Allen, Henry J.

**JEWISH SYMBOLS**
119-21                   *Bollingen Foundation

**THE JEWISH YEAR BOOK**
D15                      *Freud, Sigmund

**PRO–PALESTINE HERALD**
5                        *Holmes, John Haynes

**SH'MA**
54                       *Morgenthau, Hans J.

# III. SUBJECTS

## A. AMERICANA

This section describes manuscript collections which directly reflect the interaction between Jewish culture and American society.

**BOONE, DANIEL**

                        Receipt of Boone to Jacob Cohan (Dec. 1781)

**CROFFUT, WILLIAM A.**
29                   Yiddish poster announcing meeting of Hebrew-
p. 170             American Democratic Club, November 4, 1900, New Haven, Connecticut

**FISH, HAMILTON**
54                   Mordecai Noah's project for establishing a refuge for persecuted Jews on Grand Island, N.Y. (1/25 & 2/19/1868)

**FRANKLIN, BENJAMIN**
v. 26               Jews and anti-Federalists
p. 2275

**FRIEDMAN, HARRY T.—SPANISH AMERICAN DOCUMENTS**
3                    30 April 1865 letter in Spanish from Nahon, U.S. vice-consul in Morocco, to the U.S. consul in Morocco, expressing condolences of Jewish community over the death of Abraham Lincoln

## GERMANY—HAMBURG PASSENGER LISTS

Microfilm copies of lists of passengers embarking for America from the port of Hamburg, Germany, during the years 1850-1873. Many of these passengers are undoubtedly Jewish.

## GREAT BRITAIN, PUBLIC RECORD OFFICE, COLONIAL OFFICE 324

Vols. 55-56     Plantations General, 1740-61. "Lists of persons that have intituled themselves to the Benefit of the Act, 13 George II., for Naturalizing such Foreign Protestants and others as are settled or shall settle in any of His Majesty's Colonies in America."

Arranged by colonies, distinguishing the religion, whether Jewish or Christian, and in some cases the nationality.

## HERTZ, EMANUEL

5     Abraham Lincoln eulogies in synagogues of Cincinnati, including one by Isaac Mayer Wise

## LINCOLN, ABRAHAM

Dembitz, Louis N. (uncle of Louis D. Brandeis) August 6, 7, 8, 1861—letters regarding job references

f. 17870-71, 18878, 19222, 21026, 21089, 21159     Philadelphia Hebrew Congregation (August 21, 1862), regarding the appointment of Jewish chaplains, and follow-up letters.

f. 25134     Arrest of three Jews in July, 1863, one of whom, Abraham Lower, Jr., was a spy.

f. 37629, 37631, 37796     Isaacs, Myer W.—regarding the Jewish vote of New York City (June 26, 1864), with replies.

## LIPPINCOTT, RICHARD

Documents pertaining to his court-martial for the hanging of Joshua Huddy (1782)

## MADISON, JAMES

| | |
|---|---|
| Ser. 1 | Jacob de la Motta to Madison, regarding the consecration of the Hebrew Synagogue at Savannah, Ga., and freedom of worship in the United States (Aug. 1820) |
| v. 67 | |
| p. 108 | |

## *MEAD, MARGARET

| | |
|---|---|
| E73 | Institute of Jewish Affairs, 1941-42 |
| G44-51 | Interviews with East European refugees |
| M38 | Jews, 1944-45—studies in national character |

## MORGENTHAU, HENRY SR.

| | |
|---|---|
| 4 | Christopher Columbus and the Jews |
| 2 | Old Washingtonians "Jews and the Synagogues in the District" (1905) News clippings pertaining to the Washington Hebrew Congregation (1925)—also includes references to Mordecai M. Noah, David Yulee, Jefferson Levy, Judah P. Benjamin, Philip Phillips, A. S. Solomon, and Simon Wolf. |

## PORTER, DAVID DIXON

French Papers Claims—contain many references to business activities of Jews in Confederate States

## PUTNAM FREDERICK W.

Emanuel Hertz-Jefferson Levy correspondence regarding Jefferson's Monticello

## RANDALL, JAMES G.

| | |
|---|---|
| 16 | Lincoln and the Jews |

## *RIBICOFF, ABRAHAM A.

| | |
|---|---|
| 13 | Touro Synagogue |

## ROSENWALD, LESSING J.

| | |
|---|---|
| 8 | Abraham Lincoln and the Jews |

**RUDOLPH, CUNO H.**

Program for dedication of Jewish Foster Home in Washington, D.C. (9/29/1911)

**TONER, JOSEPH M.**

266    Lippincott, Richard—court-martial documents relating to the hanging of Joseph Huddy (1782)

**UNITED STATES WORKS PROGRESS ADMINISTRATION**

| | |
|---|---|
| A31 | California–San Francisco—Jewish culture |
| A44 | Connecticut—Ethnic survey |
| A73 | Georgia—Religion |
| A114 | Illinois—Ethnic studies—Jewish folklore—essays on cultural practices |
| A124-25 | Illinois—Religion—information on individual congregations |
| A132 | Indiana—Racial elements |
| A194 | Minnesota—Ethnic groups—Jewish |
| A517 | Illinois—Chicago–Libraries and Museums–Jewish People's Institute/Museum of Natural History |
| A542 | New York City—Temple Emanu-el |
| A550 | New York City—Jews–vivid descriptions of living conditions, area, etc. |
| A707 | Illinois—Chicago–life histories of individual Jews |
| A714 | Massachusetts—life histories of individual Jews |
| A741 | Illinois—Chicago–Jewish–essays on religious and cultural practices; life histories |
| A742 | Connecticut—Jewish–life histories of individual Jews |
| A749 | Nebraska—Jewish culture |
| A752 | New York City—Jewish culture–"Jews of New York" by Nathan Ausubel; Landsmanschaften—essays and Yiddish culture |
| A759 | Pennsylvania—Jewish culture<br>Texas—Jewish culture |

| | |
|---|---|
| A797 | New York City—*Flats and Skyscrapers* by B. Glasman, c. 1940–a novel in Yiddish |
| A811 | New York City—*Portraits of New Yorkers* |
| A862-65 | Illinois—radio scripts of many Jews |
| Historical Records Survey B22 | *Inventory of the Church and Synagogue Archives of Mississippi Jewish Congregations and Organizations* (November 1940) |
| B48-49 | Church Records Survey–District of Columbia, 1735-1941—Jewish–Congregations (Conservative, Orthodox, Reform); Directory of Jewish congregations, organizations, & associations; research materials |
| B172 | Archival & Manuscript Records–Registration of deaths—index to, 1803-60—Jewish |

## WASHINGTON, GEORGE

| | |
|---|---|
| Ser. 2 v. 39 p. 17-20 | Petition from Touro Synagogue Washington's reply to Touro—Aug. 17, 1790 (letterbook copies) |
| Ser. 3A v. 39 p. 30, 32 | Washington to Hebrew Congregations of Philadelphia, New York, Charleston, and Richmond (Dec. 13, 1790) |
| Ser. 4 v. 247 p. 41 | Petition from Touro Synagogue (Aug. 17, 1790) |
| Ser. 4 v. 240 p. 60A | Essay including comparisons between Indian languages of America and Hebrew (March 28, 1788) |

# B. ISRAEL

## 1. MIDDLE EAST

Included in this section are entries pertaining to the Middle East in general, excluding Palestine. The topics discussed in the collections cover a broad range, from political dynamics to travel accounts. This section is broader in scope than others, as it includes entries which do not directly relate to Israel, but may provide background for the scholar in search of American involvement in the area and its impact on U.S. foreign policy regarding the competing Arab and Jewish nationalist movements.

**ACKERMAN, CARL W.**
37  Egypt (1945)
    Iran (1945)

**ALLEN, HENRY J.**
C87  Near East Relief

**ALLEN, WILLIAM A. H.**
    Journals with descriptions of Egypt, Lebanon, Palestine, and Syria (1863-64)

**ALLEY, T. J.**
    "Khaleel, The Little Galilean Gleamer: A True Story of Missionary Life in the Holy Land" c. 1891

**\*ALSOP, JOSEPH AND STEWART**
57, 84  Middle East (1947 and 1956)

## AMERICAN COUNCIL OF LEARNED SOCIETIES

| | |
|---|---|
| B87 | Near Eastern studies |
| E21-22 | Committee on Near Eastern Studies |
| E79 | Emergence of Islam |
| E80 | Middle East Dictionary |
| K6 | The Arab Cause |
| | Arab Thinking Between Its Present and Past |
| | Arabic-Russian Dictionary |
| K8 | Bibliography of Survey of Persian Art |
| K9 | The Case of the Fellah |
| K10 | Development of the Feminist Movement in Egypt |
| | Development of Turkish Law |
| K10-11 | Education and Unemployment in Egypt |
| K11 | Establishment of Islam as the State Religion of Syria |
| | Future of the Arab World |
| K13-14 | History of Anglo-Iranian Relations in the 19th Century |
| K19 | Introduction to the Early History of Islam |
| | Judicial Relations Among Arab States |
| | Libya, Tunisia, and Algeria |
| K20 | The Living Arab |
| | Memoirs of Abdullah ibn al Hussain |
| | Message of Al-Azhar |
| | Mister Fahim (Bey) |
| K21 | Muhammed—A Study of His Genius |
| K22 | Near Eastern Studies in America |
| | Notables of the Near East |
| | Notables in the Middle East |
| K24 | Palestinian Parties and Politics Behind the Old Testament |
| | Politics in the Azhar |
| K29 | The Spirit of Iran |
| K34 | What the Persian Reads |
| K37 | The Future of Culture in Egypt |
| K38 | Ahmad Amin |

| | |
|---|---|
| K39 | The Development of Turkish Public Law |
| K40 | Feminist Movement in Egypt |
| | Mister Fahim (Bey) |
| K42 | Politics and the Azhar |
| | The Spirit of Iran |
| | Toward Arabic Unity |
| K43 | Turkish Short Stories |
| | What the Persian Reads |
| K46 | Turkish Word List |

**AMERICAN PEACE COMMISSION TO VERSAILLES**

| | |
|---|---|
| 34 | Syria |
| 37-38 | Algeria |
| | Arabia |
| | Egypt |
| | Palestine |
| | Sudan |
| 21, 40 | Persia |

**ANDERSON, CLINTON P.**

| | |
|---|---|
| 324 | Near East crisis (1967-68) |

**\*ARENDT, HANNAH**

| | |
|---|---|
| 18 | Plight of Syrian Jewry |

**ARNOLD, HENRY H.**

| | |
|---|---|
| 39, 152 | Middle East |
| 196 | Algiers |
| 196, 225 | Cairo |

**BATCHELDER, JOHN D.**

| | |
|---|---|
| Vol. 19 | Husein, Pasha |
| Item 760, 762 | |

**BEALE FAMILY**

| | |
|---|---|
| 2 | Diary of trip to the Middle East (1929) |

## BEER, GEORGE LOUIS

Lawrence of Arabia
Egypt
Syria

## BIGELOW, JOHN
1, 27-33, 35, 47-48

Suez Canal (19th Century)
Ancient Egypt

## BLISS, TASKER
| | |
|---|---|
| 325 | Military policy in Mesopotamia and Palestine (1918) |
| 353 | Syria (1918-19) |
| 354 | Arab state (1918-19) |
| 356 | Libya (1918-19) |
| 363 | Persia (1919) |
| | Lebanon (1919) |

## BONSAL, STEPHEN
6            Lawrence of Arabia (1919-47)

## BRISTOL, MARK L.
| | |
|---|---|
| 72 | Near East Foundation |
| 76 | Syria |
| | Post–World War I policy of the United States in the Near East |

## BROWNING FAMILY

Turkey

## BUTTERFIELD, KENYON L.
23           Near East education (1932-34)

## CARPENTER, DUDLEY N.

Journal with descriptions of the Middle East, including Egypt, Palestine, and Syria

**CELLER, EMANUEL**

| | |
|---|---|
| 250 | Iran |
| | Iraq |
| 285, 297, 501 | Arab boycott |
| 297 | Arab military policy |
| 360 | Syrian Jews and those of other Arab nations |
| 503 | Egypt (1960-68) |
| | Eisenhower Doctrine (1957) |
| 505-06 | Middle East crisis (1969-71) |

**CHAILLE-LONG, CHARLES**

Egypt and the British occupation of (1869-1912)

**CHANDLER, WILLIAM P.**

Tunis (1854-56)

**\*COHEN, BENJAMIN V.**

| | |
|---|---|
| 3-4 | Middle East conflict |

**CONFERENCE ON NEAR EASTERN AFFAIRS**

Turkey, 1922-23

**CONNALLY, THOMAS**

| | |
|---|---|
| 99-101 | Anglo-American Oil Agreement (1944-49) |
| 256 | Oil and U.S. foreign policy |
| 230 | Arab refugees (1950) |

**COTTON, CHARLES S.**

| | |
|---|---|
| 1 | Lebanon (1903) |

**CROSBY, OSCAR T.**

| | |
|---|---|
| 2, 6 | Middle East trip (1914) |

**CULBERTSON, WILLIAM S.**

| | |
|---|---|
| 131 | Middle East trip |

## DANIELS, JOSEPHUS
591                      Refugee relief work in the Near East (1915-24)
913                      Near East

## *DAVIES, JOSEPH E.
63-64                  Near and Middle East (1943-48)

## DEHAVEN, EDWIN JESSE
                             Turkey (1843)

## DENNY, GEORGE V.
4                           Proposal for interview with Ben-Gurion and Nasser, entitled "What Basis for Peace in the Middle East"

## DERRICK, HENRY CLAY
                             Egypt—Diaries (1875-1878) kept while under the service of the Khedive as an engineer and chief engineer of the Egyptian Army

## DRAMA AND THEATRE
                             "Asshur Prince of Shomer or Smiles and Tears" c. 1890

## DUNCAN, GEORGE STEWART
                             Egypt—archaeology

## DURANT, WILLIAM H.
                             Materials in Turkish and Arabic, pertaining to business trips in the Middle East

## EAKER, IRA C.
7-8                      Middle East & World War II (1944)

## FLETCHER, HENRY P.
13                        Morocco, 1926

**FORCE, PETER**
**(SERIES 8D—WYVILL, RICHARD A. PAPERS)**
　　　　　　　　　　Egypt (19th Century)

**FOULKE, WILLIAM DUDLEY**
　　　　　　　　　　Middle East Trips

**\*GARMENT, LEONARD**
6　　　　　　　　　Middle East, 1973-74

**GILCHREST, HUNTINGTON**
20　　　　　　　　Arab press (1929)
　　　　　　　　　British Near East mandates (1920-26)
26　　　　　　　　Reports by Mandatory Powers:
　　　　　　　　　France on Syria
　　　　　　　　　Britain on Palestine and Trans-Jordan
　　　　　　　　　Syria (1925-26)

**GOSNELL, HAROLD**
1　　　　　　　　　CIA—Egypt, 1956-1957

**GREEN, THEODORE FRANCIS**
　　　　　　　　　Trips to the Middle East
　　　　　　　　　U.S. policy towards the Middle East

**GRISWOLD, RALPH E.**
4-8　　　　　　　　Egypt and the Near East, including brochures, maps, and photos

**HACKWORTH, GREEN H.**
6　　　　　　　　　Israel and the Suez War of 1956
　　　　　　　　　United Arab Republic (1960)

**\*HAIG, ALEXANDER**
　　　　　　　　　U.S. policy toward the Middle East

**HARBORD, JAMES G.**
　　　　　　　　　Post–World War I policy of the United States toward the Middle East

## SUBJECTS

**HARDING, WARREN G.**
                        Near East Relief

**HARRIS, WILLIAM TORREY**
44-45                Persia

**HARRISON, LELAND**
8                      Near Eastern division
104                  Syrian anti-Zionist propaganda
105                  Cherif Pasha

**\*HENDERSON, LOY W.**
9                      Iran, 1954-78
10                   Iraq, 1943-68
12                   Middle East oil, 1943
                       Near Eastern Affairs, 1945-48

**HOOPER, STANFORD C.**
                       Post–World War I policy of the United States toward the Middle East

**HOWARD, ROY**
285                  Middle East articles (1955)

**HUGHES, CHARLES EVANS**
174                  Egypt (1921-25)
176                  Persia

**HULL, CORDELL**
28                   Egypt (1935-44)
30                   Iran (1935-44)
                       Iraq (1942-43)
85                   Petroleum—United States policy (1939-47)

**HUTCHISON, RALPH WALDO**
                       Iran, oil, and the Middle East

## ICKES, HAROLD L.

| | |
|---|---|
| Diaries | Arab concerns of Jewish colonization of Palestine |
| 44 | Arabs (1952) |
| 45 | Aviation in the Middle East (1946) |
| 67 | Iran (1946-51) |
| 75 | Oil (1946-52) |
| 76 | Palestine (1946-50) |
| 159 | Foreign oil policy (1943) |

## INMAN, SAMUEL GUY

| | |
|---|---|
| 43 | Mid-East |

## INTER-PARLIAMENTARY UNION

| | |
|---|---|
| 8 | Iraq |

## *JACKSON, ROBERT H.

| | |
|---|---|
| 100 | Grand Mufti of Jerusalem (Haj Amin El-Husseini) |

## JARDINE, WILLIAM M.

| | |
|---|---|
| | Egypt (1930-33) |

## JESSUP, PHILIP P.

| | |
|---|---|
| 16 | Egypt |
| | Morocco |
| | Sudan |
| | Tunisia |
| 18 | Iraq |
| | Middle Eastern cities |
| 32 | Middle East |
| 77-78 | Middle East trip (1956) |
| 152 | Near East (1943) |
| 157 | Pact of League of Arab states (1945) |

## *KISSINGER, HENRY A.

    1973 War and its aftermath—
    —Egypt
    —Iraq
    —Israel
    —Jordan
    —Kuwait
    —Lebanon
    —Libya
    —Morocco
    —Oman
    —Palestinians
    —PLO
    —Syria
    —Soviet Union
    —Yemen

## LANDIS, JAMES M.

| | |
|---|---|
| 31-32 | Arab-American Oil Company—Lend Lease (1947-50) |
| 56 | Middle East Oil Company (1948-50) |
| | *Middle East Economist* |
| 119 | Middle East |

## LANSING, ROBERT

    Middle East
    Anglo-Persian Agreement (1919)
    Counsel for Persia (1921)
    Oil

## LEAR, TOBIAS

    Algiers (c. 1810)

## *LUCE, CLARE BOOTHE

| | |
|---|---|
| B489 | Iran |
| 514 | Middle East (1940) |
| 515 | Arab-Jewish and Palestine question |
| | Iraq |

**LEAHY, WILLIAM D.**
4-6 U.S. Middle East policy

**MAC VEAGH, FRANKLIN**
31 Egypt (1884-1923)

***MALIK, CHARLES H.**
| | |
|---|---|
| I 5 | American Middle East relief |
| I 48 | Iraq, Jordan |
| I 35, 51-55 | Lebanon |
| I 55 | Libya |
| I 60 | Morocco |
| I 78 | Saudi Arabia |
| I 82 | Sudan |
| I 83 | Syria, Egypt |
| I 85 | Turkey |
| I 86 | United Arab Republic |
| II 13, 18 | United Nations—Lebanon |

**MASON, ALEXANDER MACOMB**
Egypt and Sudan (1871-98)

***MEAD, MARGARET**
| | |
|---|---|
| G59-61 | Interviews with Syrian refugees |
| K64 | Iran, 1974-76 |
| O82 | Syria—Projects in Contemporary Cultures |

**MONTGOMERY FAMILY**
2 Middle East
King-Crane Commission

**MORAL RE-ARMAMENT**
| | |
|---|---|
| 137 | Egypt (1941-52) |
| 141 | Iran (1953-60) |
| 183 | Islam |
| 186 | Iraq |

| | |
|---|---|
| 253 | Middle East (1954-64) |
| 302 | Egypt (1940-55) |
| 316 | Iran (1949-63) |
| | Iraq (1955) |
| 328 | Middle East (1953-54) |

**\*MORGENTHAU, HANS J.**

|  | Arab-Israeli conflict |
|---|---|
| 92 | Libya, 1963-79 |

**MORGENTHAU, HENRY SR.**

Near East relief

**\*MOYNIHAN, DANIEL PATRICK**

U.S. policy in the United Nations toward Israel and the Middle East

**NATIONAL COUNCIL OF JEWISH WOMEN—WASHINGTON, D.C. OFFICE**

| 195 | Middle East |
|---|---|
| 197 | Near East Report |

**\*NIEBUHR, REINHOLD**

| 16 | Middle East |
|---|---|

**NIELSON, FREDERICK K.**

U.S.-Egyptian relations

**OPPENHEIMER, J. ROBERT**

| 62 | Bertrand Russell on the danger of nuclear war in the Middle East (1963) |
|---|---|

**\*OSBORNE, JOHN**

Dayan, Moshe
Sadat, Anwar

**PATTERSON, DANIEL TODD**

Turkey (c. 1820)

**\*PATTON, GEORGE S.**
54                                  Arabs, 1943

**PINCHOT, AMOS**
77                                  Egypt (notes—11/16/1926, regarding its independence and its relationship with Britain)

**\*PODHORETZ, NORMAN**
1                                   Peace in the Middle East—See Perlmutter, Nathan (1982), etc.
8                                   "AWACS"—1981
10                                  "J'Accuse"—1982
                                    (War in Lebanon)
                                    "The Massacre: Who Was Responsible"—1982
                                    (War in Lebanon)
11                                  "Our Aims and Israel's"—1982
                                    (War in Lebanon)

**PORTER, DAVID DIXON**
                                    Turkey (1820's–1830's)

**PREBLE, EDWARD**
                                    Algiers (c. 1800)

**\*RIBICOFF, ABRAHAM A.**
422-26                              Middle East (1967-80)
582                                 Middle East trip (1976)
653                                 Libya

**ROBERTS, EDMUND**
                                    Travels in the Middle East (1820's–1830's)

**ROOSEVELT, KERMIT**
                                    U.S. policy in the Middle East

**ROSENWALD, LESSING J.**
2                                   Observations of Egypt—1937
9                                   Need for peaceful solution in the Near East

## SANGER, MARGARET

| | |
|---|---|
| 19 | Egypt (1934-37) |
| 29 | Persia (1936-37) |
| | Palestine (1928-37) |
| 31 | Syria (1934) |

## SAYRE, FRANCIS B.

| | |
|---|---|
| 10-11 | UNNRA—Egypt, Iran, Iraq |

## SCHUYLER, EUGENE

| | |
|---|---|
| | Turkey (1876-78) |

## SCOTT, CHARLES L.

| | |
|---|---|
| 7 | Middle East—reports on operations (1940-45) |
| 9 | Middle East—photographs (1940-45) |

## SIMONS, WILLIAM H.

| | |
|---|---|
| 5 | Palestine |

## SOBELOFF, SIMON E.

| | |
|---|---|
| 15 | Displaced persons (1947-52) |

## SPIVAK, LAWRENCE E.

| | |
|---|---|
| 233 | Eban, Abba |
| | Hussein, King |
| 234 | Dayan, Moshe |
| 236 | Begin, Menachem |
| 240 | Weizman, Ezer |
| 243 | Sadat, Anwar |
| 244 | Peres, Shimon |
| 245 | Arafat, Yasser |
| 246 | Israel |
| |   Meir, Golda |
| |   Allon, Yigal |
| |   Eban, Abba |
| 250 | Hussein, King |

**STEINHARDT, LAURENCE A.**
45, etc. Middle East
Turkey and its policies towards Jews

**TERHUNE, ALBERT P.**
Travels in Syria and Jordan (1894)

**TAFT, CHARLES P.**
153 Arab/Israel
155 Egypt
159 Middle East

**TAFT, ROBERT A.**
736 Palestine refugees (1950)

**TAFT, WILLIAM HOWARD**
Near East relief

**TERRETT, COLVILLE**
Middle Eastern ports

**THAYER, WILLIAM S.**
Egyptian-U.S. relations

**TURKEY MISCELLANY**
Surrender of Jerusalem by Izat Bey (Dec. 8-9, 1917)

**UNITED STATES WORKS PROGRESS ADMINISTRATION**
A739 Illinois-Chicago—Assyrian essays
A741 Illinois-Chicago—Persian essays
A748 Foreign press—Arabic

**VON NEUMANN, JOHN**
37 Scrapbook with photographs of Turkey

## WARREN, EARL

| | |
|---|---|
| 59 | Middle East, 1963 |
| 60 | Iran, Lebanon, 1963 |
| 61 | Turkey, United Arab Republic, 1963 |
| 62 | Near East, 1969 |
| 116 | Ethiopia, Morocco |

## WASHINGTON, GEORGE THOMAS

Iran, Iraq, and post–World War II policies of the United States in the Near East

## *WEINBERGER, CASPAR

Middle East

## WELSH, GEORGE P.

Middle Eastern ports

## WHITE, THOMAS

46  Middle East

## WILSON, WOODROW

Middle East

## YARD, EDWARD M.

Middle Eastern ports

# 2. PALESTINE

Because of Palestine's importance in Jewish history and the Middle East equation in general, this section is devoted solely to entries which refer directly to Palestine. Palestine, for the purposes of this guide, is defined as that area under the control of the Ottoman Empire and succeeded by Great Britain during the mandatory period.

## ABDUL BAHA

Palestine, 1930-32

**ACKERMAN, CARL W.**
37 Palestine (1945)

**ALLEN, WILLIAM A. H.**
Journals with descriptions of Palestine (1863-64)

**AMERICAN PEACE COMMISSION TO VERSAILLES**
1, 34, 37-8, 40 Palestine

**ARNOLD, HENRY H.**
25 American Palestine Aviation Society (4/23/1948)

**BEER, GEORGE LOUIS**
Palestine

**BLISS, TASKER H.**
362 Palestine (1919)

**BORAH, WILLIAM E.**
119 Palestine (1921-22)
513 Palestine—Jews (1939)

**CELLER, EMANUEL**
23-30 Israel/Palestine (1929-36)
346 Israel (1971-72)
501-08 Israel (1944-71)

**\*COHEN, BENJAMIN V.**
2, 4, 12 Palestine

**CONRAD, DANIEL B.**
Journal which includes entries on visit to Jerusalem (1857)

**DANIELS, JOSEPHUS**
524 Relief of starving Jews in Palestine

## DICKINSON, CHARLES M.
Investigation of U.S. consuls in Smyrna and Jerusalem

## EAKER, IRA C.
7                      Observations of trip to Jerusalem (4/27/44)

## *FEIS, HERBERT
28-31, 87-92         Palestine

## FISH, HAMILTON
60                  Protection of Jews in Turkish Palestine

## FRANKFURTER, FELIX
28, 40, 161-62       Palestine

## GILCHREST, HUNTINGTON
26                  Reports by Mandatory powers—Britain on Palestine

## GOLDENWEISER, EMANUEL A.
5                      Palestine and Anglo-Palestine Bank (1947-49)

## GRANIK, SAMUEL THEODORE
28                  Palestine Foundation Fund

## *HENDERSON, LOY
11-12               Israel-Palestine

## HOWARD, ROY
Palestine and the MIddle East

## HULL, CORDELL
51                  "A Plan for Peace in the Near East" (3/20/43)
59                  Statements regarding Jewish situation in Palestine, including immigration and relief (1942-1943)
66                  British policy regarding Jewish immigration to Palestine (9/1/36)

**ICKES, HAROLD L.**
Diaries                    Palestine (1946-50)

**KENNAN, GEORGE L.**
                           Number of Jews inhabiting Palestine

**\*LA FOLLETTE FAMILY**
C57                        Palestine (1945)
C417                       Jewish-Palestine Lend-Lease Bill

**LANSING, ROBERT**
14                         Jewish problem—Palestine (1915)
37                         "British Justice in Palestine"
40                         Zionism

**LEAHY, WILLIAM D.**
4-6                        Palestine

**LIBBY, FREDERICK J.**
1                          Palestine trip (1909)

**LONG, BRECKINRIDGE**
199                        Near Eastern Affairs (1941-44)
200                        Palestine (1944)

**\*MALIK, CHARLES H.**
I 67                       Palestine
II 9                       United Nations—Palestine problem

**\*MEAD, MARGARET**
M38                        Jews, 1944-45—studies in national character—includes material regarding Palestine and Zionism

**\*MORGENTHAU, HANS J.**
                           Palestine problem

## MORGENTHAU, HENRY SR.
19, etc.            Palestine

## NATIONAL COUNCIL OF JEWISH WOMEN—WASHINGTON, D.C. OFFICE
Palestine

## *NIEBUHR, REINHOLD
25            Anglo-American Commission of Inquiry on Palestine (1946)

## ORR, WILLIAM
5            Palestine and the Near East

## PASVOLSKY, LEO
1            International economic relations and Palestine (1943)

## *PATTERSON, ROBERT P.
20-21            Problems with Jews in post-War refugee camps and possible emigration to Palestine

## *RIBICOFF, ABRAHAM A.
3            Palestine

## ROSENWALD, LESSING J.
5            Request for Jewish-Arab cooperation in Palestine
Terrorism
Woodhead Commission
Palestine Economic Corporation
Upbuilding of Palestine—1945
6            Palestine
7            Jewish-Arab conflict, including reports of American Friends Service Mission to Palestine (1948), containing vivid descriptions of fighting and a visit of King Abdullah to Jerusalem
Aaron Aaronsohn and agriculture
8            Gaza Strip and Palestinian refugees

## RUSSELL, CHARLES EDWARD
33 Palestine mandate (1933)

## RUSSIAN ORTHODOX GREEK CATHOLIC CHURCH IN ALASKA
(Alaska Russian Church)
| | |
|---|---|
| D24 | Palestine Mission (1904) |
| D61 | Palestine Mission (1900-11) |
| D116 | Palestine Mission (1879-1905) |
| D145 | Palestine Mission (1895-1905) |
| D159 | Palestine Mission (1887-1904) |
| D192 | Palestine Mission (1860-1913) |
| D229 | Palestine Mission (1902-04) |
| D258 | Palestine Mission (1899-1904) |
| D278 | Palestine Mission (1865-1905) |
| D321 | Palestine Mission (1877-1905) |
| D326 | Palestine Mission (1897-1905) |
| D331 | Palestine Mission (1899-1903) |
| D374 | Palestine Mission (1842-1909) |

## SANGER, MARGARET
29 Palestine (1928-37)

## SAYRE, FRANCIS B.
13 Palestine

## STRAUS, OSCAR S.
Palestine

## SWEETSER, ARTHUR
75 Palestine (1937-38)

## TALMADGE, THOMAS DEWITT
3 Diary of Holy Land trip (1890)

## TAFT, ROBERT A.
733-35, 878, 909, 1027, 1056   Palestine

**TAFT, WILLIAM HOWARD**
                    Palestine Restoration Fund

# 3. ZIONISM

Included under this heading are manuscripts pertaining directly to the Zionist movement itself, its leaders, its adherents and opponents, and its organizational structure.

**AMERICAN PEACE COMMISSION TO VERSAILLES**
1, 34                Palestine/Zionism

**\*ARENDT, HANNAH**
56                  "The Crisis of Zionism" (1943)
63                  Zionism
72                  "Zionism Reconsidered" (1945)
                    "Der Zionismus aus Heutiger Sicht" (1945)

**BLISS, TASKER**
354                Arab state
358                Jewish question and Zionism (1919)
362                Palestine

**BORAH, WILLIAM E.**
498                Jewish affairs (1938)

**BRANDEIS, LOUIS**
                    Jewish Agency

**CARNEGIE ANDREW**
304                Henry S. Pritchett—Zionist Movement in Palestine, 1926-33 (File 912)

**CELLER, EMANUEL**
23-30              Israel
41                  Herzl, Theodor
                    Zionist organization

| | |
|---|---|
| 51 | Weizmann, Chaim |
| 501-08 | Israel |

**\*COHEN, BENJAMIN V.**
| | |
|---|---|
| 3 | Zionist history |

**CULBERTSON, WILLIAM**
| | |
|---|---|
| 25 | Formation of Jewish state |

**DIXON, FREDERICK**
| | |
|---|---|
| 1-2 | Establishment of home for Jews in Palestine (c. 1920) |

**FRANKFURTER, FELIX**
| | |
|---|---|
| 125 | Aaronsohn, Aaron |
| 26-9, 115, 128, 161-62 | Brandeis, Louis |
| 23 | Ben-Gurion, David |
| 40 | Buxton, Frank |
| 52 | Eban, Abba |
| 162 | Palestine—Zionism |
| 202 | Weizmann, Chaim |
| 205 | Frankfurter's views on Zionism |

**FRANKFURTER ZIONISM COLLECTION**

    Four reels of microfilm, reproducing the subject file on Zionism, the originals of which were transferred to Israel

**\*HENDERSON, LOY W.**
| | |
|---|---|
| 11-12 | Israel-Palestine |
| 12 | Near Eastern Affairs, 1945-48 |

**\*HOLMES, JOHN HAYNES**
| | |
|---|---|
| 5 | Pro–Palestinian Herald |

**ICKES, HAROLD L.**
| | |
|---|---|
| Diaries | Jews—settlement of in various lands, including Palestine |

## *LUCE, CLARE BOOTHE
| | |
|---|---|
| B514 | Palestine—national home for the Jews |
| | Zionism |
| 515 | Arab/Jewish and Palestine question |
| | Israel—radio broadcasts (1947) |

## MOORE, JOHN BASSETT
| | |
|---|---|
| 158 | Jews (1917-41) |

## *MORGENTHAU, HANS J.
Zionism

## MORGENTHAU, HENRY SR.
| | |
|---|---|
| 9, 22 | Zionism |

## NATIONAL CIVIC FEDERATION
References to Theodor Herzl and Zionism

## NATIONAL COUNCIL OF JEWISH WOMEN—WASHINGTON, D.C. OFFICE
| | |
|---|---|
| 221 | Zionism (1977) |
| | United Nations and Zionism (1977) |

## ROSENWALD, LESSING J.
| | |
|---|---|
| | Anti-Zionist views |
| 4 | Zionism in the U.S.—1944 |
| 5 | Hebrew Union College and Zionism |
| 6, 8 | Zionism in the U.S. and abroad |
| 9 | American Council for Judaism and Zionism |

## RUSSELL, CHARLES EDWARD
| | |
|---|---|
| 18 | Hadassah comments on speech about Zionism and other topics |
| 21 | Jewish homeland—letters with Taraknath Das and John Haynes Holmes about recruiting the aid of De Valera and Gandhi (Oct. 17-18, 1938) |
| 33 | Palestine mandate |
| 38 | Zionism |

**SOBELOFF, SIMON E.**
15                          American Zionist Council—Zionism/Israel

**STRAUS, OSCAR S.**
                            Zionism

**TAYLOR, MYRON**
Box 2                       Pope's views on the future of Palestine, includ-
V. 1 (1943)                 ing a 3/6/22 report on the British mandate of
6/24/43                     Palestine

**UNITED STATES WORKS PROGRESS ADMINISTRATION**
A114                        Illinois—Chicago
                            Ethnic Studies
                            Jewish Culture
                            Zionism in Chicago

**WILSON, WOODROW**
Ser. 4                      Jews (1913-20)—includes correspondence from
Case file 618               de Haas, Wise, etc.
                            Weizmann, Chaim
                            Wise, Stephen S.

**WOOLEY, ROBERT W.**
40                          "Zionist Men of Wisdom" (1919)

# 4. MISCELLANY

This section contains a potpourri of information, including collections on the formation of Israel as a modern state, its growing relations with the world community, and its cultural development.

**BERKNER, LLOYD V.**
22                          Israel conference (1960)

**CARNEGIE, ANDREW**
304                         Judah Magnes—Israel

## SUBJECTS

**CELLER, EMANUEL**
346   Israel (1971-72)

**\*COHEN, BENJAMIN V.**
2, 4, 12   Israel

**DAVIDSON, JO**
Sculpture File   Israel

**\*DOUGLAS, WILLIAM O.**
II-9   Israel Bonds, 1964-70
Israeli Ambassador's Ball, 1960-74

**DREIKURS, RUDOLF**
4   Israel
Israeli Air Force Technical School

**\*FEIS, HERBERT**
79, 88   *The Birth of Israel*

**FRANFURTER, FELIX**
149   Israel Philharmonic Orchestra (1951)
Israeli Embassy (1954-55, 1959)
212   Israel's 10th Anniversary: Speech (1958)

**\*GARMENT, LEONARD**
5   Israel, 1973

**GITELSON, MAXWELL**
78   Israel—Jerusalem (1963-64)

**HACKWORTH, GREEN H.**
6   Israel and Bulgaria (1955)

**HINES, LEWIS G.**
18   AF of L—Jews (1944)

**ICKES, HAROLD L.**
67 Israel (1949-50)
372 "Messiah's Government Herald the New Jewish State" (10/2/1940)

**INMAN, SAMUEL GUY**
38 Israel
39 Jerusalem survey

**INTER–PARLIAMENTARY UNION**
8 Israel

**KANIN, GARSON**
4 Israeli production of Born Yesterday

**KLEIN, JULIUS**
Opening of diplomatic relations between Israel and West Germany

**\*MALIK, CHARLES H.**
I 48 Israel
Jerusalem, internationalization of
II 8 United Nations—Israel, admission to (1949)
II 9 United Nations—Jerusalem, internationalization of

**\*MEAD, MARGARET**
M34 Israel—Studies in national character
M38 Jews, 1944-45—Studies in national character

**MERRIAM, C. HART**
69 Israel

**MEYER, AGNES**
36 State of Israel Bonds (1960)
51, 61 Israel

**MEYER, EUGENE**
45                      Israel

**MOORE, JOHN BASSETT**
158                     Jews (1917-41)

***MORGENTHAU, HANS J.**
91                      Israel, 1955-80

**NATIONAL COUNCIL OF JEWISH WOMEN—WASHINGTON, D.C. OFFICE**
29                      Embassy of Israel

**OPPENHEIMER, J. ROBERT**
40                      Israel (1958)

***PODHORETZ, NORMAN**
1                       America-Israel Cultural Foundation
2                       Amin, Idi,—African-Israeli relations

**RANDOLPH, A. PHILIP**
23                      Israel, 1964-75

**RAPAPORT, DAVID**
37-8                    Israel

**REID FAMILY**
D230-31                 Israel

***RIBICOFF, ABRAHAM A.**
2                       Israel

**ROSENWALD, LESSING J.**
7                       Support of Israel—1948
8                       Relations with Arabs and conditions following the War of Independence
9                       Peter Bergson and Middle East Industries, Inc.—1951

|   |   |
|---|---|
|   | American Fund for Israel Institutions and the museums of Israel—1951 |
| 49 | Committee for Justice and Peace in the Holy Land |
| 58 | UJA's Study Mission to Israel and Paris—1970 |

**SOBELOFF, SIMON E.**

| | |
|---|---|
| 351 | American Christian Palestine Committee |
| 360 | Materials for Israel, Inc. |
| 393 | Travels—Israel, 1955 |

**SPIVAK, LAWRENCE E.**

| | |
|---|---|
| 30 | Ben-Gurion, David |
| 92 | Israel special (May 6, 1973) |

**TAFT, CHARLES P.**

| | |
|---|---|
| 94, 158 | Israel |

**TAFT, ROBERT A.**

| | |
|---|---|
| 307, 667, 918, 988 | Israel |

**UNITED NATIONS—PALESTINE PARTITION RESOLUTION**

|   |   |
|---|---|
|   | Voting sheet of, autographed by many principals (11/29/47) |

**WARREN, EARL**

| | |
|---|---|
| 59 | Israel, 1962 |
| 61 | Israel, 1966 |

# C. JUDAICA

Materials directly related to Judaism and Jewish culture are included in this section.

## 1. BIBLICAL

**AMERICAN COUNCIL OF LEARNED SOCIEITES**
B51 Hebrew biblical project

**BLISS, TASKER**
382 Military study: Joshua and Moses

**BRYAN, WILLIAM JENNINGS**
35 Prophecy and the Bible (4/4/22)

**DUNCAN, GEORGE S.**
 Biblical archaeology and religion throughout the Middle East

**FREY, JOHN P.**
29 Speech—"The First Temple in Jerusalem" (1953)

**MC VAY, CHARLES B. JR.**
3 "New Proofs of Old Testament History"

**SCHILLER, JOHANN CHRISTIAN FREDERICH VON**
 "The Mission of Moses" ("Die Sendung Moses")

**UNITED STATES WORKS PROGRESS ADMINISTRATION**
A114                Illinois—Chicago
                    Ethnic Studies
                    Jewish Culture
                        Biblical legends
                        Esther
                        Talmud

**ZAPPULA, FRANK S.**
                    "Solomon's Temple"—poem

## 2. LITERATURE

**AMERICAN COUNCIL OF LEARNED SOCIETIES**
B14                 Bibliography of Jewish history and literature

**BLACKWELL FAMILY**
33-4                Hebrew poems

**\*MICHENER, JAMES**
91-102              *The Source*
126                 "Noble Jerusalem"

**PHILLIPS, PHILIP FAMILY**
22                  "Vindiciae Judaeorum" (1861) by Jacob C. Levy

## 3. MUSIC

**DOCK, LAVINIA L.**
                    Note (3/6/1942) regarding Felix Mendelssohn's oratorio "The Elijah"

## 4. RELIGION

**FURMAN, BESS**
45                      Judaism

**MERVINE, THOMAS**
                       Note on marble stone containing Hebrew letters

**ROSENWALD, LESSING J.**
8                       Yom Kippur broadcast, 1949, from the Hebrew Union College/Jewish Institute of Religion

                       Dropsie College—important institute for scholarship on American Judaism

**RUSSELL, CHARLES EDWARD**
21
p. 4058              Proposed revival of Jewish proselytizing by Gentiles (1938)

**SANGER, MARGARET**
231                    Church and religion—Jewish (1932-33)

**TAFT, CHARLES P.**
94                      Judaism

**UNITED STATES WORKS PROGRESS ADMINISTRATION**
                       Illinois—Chicago
A114                  Ethnic Studies
                         Jewish Culture
                         Kashrut and hygiene
                         Marriage
                         Prayer
                         Ritual
                         Women

# D. MISCELLANY

All entries in this section refer only generally to Jews or Jewish concerns.

**ALLEN, FRED**
                      Radio scripts including Minnie Nussbaum and her Yiddish humor

**\*ARENDT, HANNAH**
53                    Jews, 1969-75
61                    Jews and the state

**\*BERNAYS, EDWARD L.**
13                    Jewish affairs, 1945

**\*BLACK, HUGO L.**
249-50              Supreme Court, Nomination File—Jewish

**BORAH, WILLIAM**
468, 490-91        Jews (Foreign Affairs, 1937-38)

**BRAZIL**
1                     Jews during the Dutch occupation of Brazil (c. 1650)

**CATT, CARRIE CHAPMAN**
14                    American Hebrew Medal

**CELLER, EMANUEL**
23                    "The Future of Indian Jewry," 1947
346                 Jews

## SUBJECTS

**CLAPPER, RAYMOND**
160                    Jews, 1939

**FISH, HAMILTON**
87                      Mercantile tendency of modern Jew (5/3/1872)

**GARMENT, LEONARD**
5                       Jewish matters, 1969-74

**GLEASON, ARTHUR H.**
                       Status of Jews in America

**\*HOLMES, JOHN HAYNES**
17                      Jewish

**ICKES, HAROLD L.**
Diaries, 68             Jews, 1946-48

**KENNAN, GEORGE L.**
108-10                Jews—emigration, condition, character, agriculture, employment, ritual murder, etc.

**MEYER, AGNES**
36                      Jews, 1965

**MEYER, EUGENE**
45                      Miscellaneous Jewish organizations

**MOORE, JOHN BASSETT**
158                    Jews, 1917-41

**\*MORGENTHAU, HANS J.**
31                      Jewish minorities research, 1962-78
91                      Hebrew School course in Jewish institutions, 1938
192                    German and Jewish materials, ca. 1920-40

## *NAACP
IIA-330 Jews, 1940-55
IIIB-135 Jews, 1956-57

## NATIONAL BOARD FOR HISTORICAL SERVICE
11 Jews

## NATIONAL COUNCIL OF JEWISH WOMEN—WASHINGTON, D.C. OFFICE
Office Files — Contemporary Jewish affairs
Quality of Jewish life
58 National Jewish community relations

## PAUL WILKINSON—INDIAN LANGUAGES
24 Medicina Maya—Libro de Judio de Solola (Ac. 4056)
Libro de Judio, 1797-1802
—Mexico-Yucatan (Ac. 1636) (1883 copy)

## *PODHORETZ, NORMAN
1, 12 American-Jewish social history

## PORTUGUESE MANUSCRIPTS
541 Document to a Jew, Jose Canica, concerning a vineyard (Sept. 30, 1428)

## RIIS, JACOB
6 On Jews

## ROSENWALD, LESSING J.
1-6, 8-9, 34, 39, 58 Jewish philanthropy

## ROOSEVELT, THEODORE
Ser. 5A Duty of the Jews
Ser. 2, pt. 2 p. 917-19 — Roosevelt statement on Jewish policy in letter of May 5, 1901, to George Briggs Aiton

## RUSSELL, CHARLES EDWARD
46                      "Portrait of Jewess"

## SHAPIRO, KARL JAY
11                      "An American Jewish Writer Looks Around"

## TAFT, ROBERT A.
307, 455, 876, 888,      Jewish
897, 907, 919, 988,
1127, 1233

## WILSON, WOODROW

                       Algerian Jews (see Tubian, Henry)
Ser. 4                 Jews, 1913-20
Case file 618

# E. PERSECUTION

It is an unfortunate reality that one of the largest subject categories of this guide must be devoted to the various forms and phases of the persecution of Jewry. From anti-Semitism in general, to the Spanish Inquisition in Mexico, and through the Holocaust and the persecution of Soviet Jewry, the following sections list collections which may provide the reader with information concerning some of the most notorious aspects, incidents, and figures of these gruesome chapters of Jewish history.

## 1. ANTI-SEMITISM

**"ANTISEMITISMUS"**

German essay defending anti-Semitism (1932)

**\*ARENDT, HANNAH**

| | |
|---|---|
| 18 | Oberammergau Passion Play |
| 60 | Anti-Semitism in France and in Germany |
| 61 | Dreyfus affair |
| 63, 74 | Sur L'Antisemitisme, 1972-73 |

**BELL, ALEXANDER GRAHAM**

| | |
|---|---|
| 61 | Drafts of articles—<br>"The Dreyfus Case"<br>"Dreyfus" |

**BONSAL, STEPHEN**

| | |
|---|---|
| 3 | Van Loon, Heinrik Willen (c. 1944) |

**BORAH, WILLIAM E.**

| | |
|---|---|
| 490 | Anti-Semitism in the U.S. |

## SUBJECTS

**BROTHERHOOD OF SLEEPING CAR PORTERS**
Black-Jewish relations

**BRYAN, WILLIAM JENNINGS**
37                  Henry Ford and the Jews (3/10/23)

**BUCK, SOLON J.**
40                  "Secret Rulers Exposed by the Chicago Tribune"
folder G

**CELLER, EMANUEL**
37                  Discrimination against U.S. Jews
245                Bombings of synagogues
263                Anti-Semitism
284                American Nazi Party (1960-61)
288                Anti-Semitism abroad
309                Anti-Semitism in New York (1968-70)

**CLAPPER, RAYMOND**
160                Jews, 1939—anti-Semitism in America

**DANIELS, JOSEPHUS**
524                Henry Ford's dissemination of anti-Semitic views

**DAVIS, ELMER**
1                   Anti-Semitism in the U.S.

**FLANNER-SOLANO**
5                   Anti-Semitic political cartoon
folder: de Gaulle

**FRANKFURTER, FELIX**
126                Anti-Semitism (1922, 1934-45)

**\*GARMENT, LEONARD**
5                   Anti-semitism

**\*HOLMES, JOHN HAYNES**
10, 14                 Anti-Defamation League

**HOWARD, ROY**
                       Editorial policy in handling anti-Semitism in Germany and its ramifications for U.S. readership

**HUEBSCH, BENJAMIN W.**
                       Black-Jewish relations

**ICKES, HAROLD L.**
Diary                 German-American anti-Semitism
                       Increase in anti-Semitism in the U.S.
                       Lindbergh and anti-Semitism
                       Spread of anti-Semitism among Negroes
                       Statements by Ickes and Joseph Kennedy
                       Opposition to Felix Frankfurter's Supreme Court nomination

**\*JACKSON, ROBERT H.**
                       Pre–World War II anti-Semitic propaganda
52                       "Anti-Semitism"—1939
78                       Anti-Semitic propaganda

**LEADERSHIP CONFERENCE ON CIVIL RIGHTS**
163                     National Conference of Jewish Women
169                     Black and Jewish relationships

**LONG, BRECKINRIDGE**
177                     Theodore Roosevelt on religious prejudices

**MOSELEY, GEORGE VAN HORN**
2, 5                    Anti-Semitic views of a high-ranking U.S. Army officer, 1933-1939

## *NAACP

| | |
|---|---|
| I, C, 208 | Anti-Semitism (1935-38) |
| I, H, 11 | |
| I, C, 277 | Discrimination—Jews (1939) |
| II, A, 71 | Anti-Semitism |
| II, Addenda, 7 | Anti-Semitism (1935-39) |
| III, B, 135 | Jews (1956-57) |

## NATIONAL CIVIC FEDERATION

Combatting anti-Semitism in the 1920's–1930's, with references to "Protocols of Zion" and Henry Ford, as well as inferences of Jews being part of the international Communist conspiracy.

## NATIONAL COUNCIL OF JEWISH WOMEN—WASHINGTON, D.C. OFFICE

| | |
|---|---|
| Alpha. and Working File | Jewish issue |
| 221 | Zionism |
| | United Nations and Zionism as racism (1977) |
| Alpha. and Working File | Anti-Defamation League |

## *NATIONAL URBAN LEAGUE

Black-Jewish relations

## PINFOLD, CHARLES

| | |
|---|---|
| 95 | Laws of Barbados—Acts of Assembly, 1643-1762 |
| | Aug. 10, 1681—petition of several Hebrews of Barbados complaining of injuries in commerce |

## *PODHORETZ, NORMAN

| | |
|---|---|
| 2 | Amin, Idi, 1975—Black-Jewish relations |

## RANDOLPH, A. PHILIP

Black-Jewish relations

**RAPAPORT, DAVID**
II, 27 Notes on anti-Semitism

**ROSENWALD, LESSING J.**
2 Reference to anti-Semitic views of Gen. George van Horn Moseley (5/29/39)
3, 8 Anti-Semitism in the U.S.

**RUSSELL, CHARLES EDWARD**
37 "On Anti-Semitism"

**\*SPINGARN, ARTHUR B.**
Black-Jewish relationships

**STRAUS, OSCAR S.**
Anti-Jewish feeling

**TAFT, ROBERT A.**
487-88 Anti-Jewish propaganda

**TAYLOR, MYRON**
Box 5A Anti-Jewish feelings in U.S. dioceses
v. 2 (1940-45)
Pt. I—2/13/40

# 2. HOLOCAUST

## a. Concentration Camps

**\*ARENDT, HANNAH**
64 *Auschwitz*

**CARNEGIE, ANDREW**
304 Judah Magnes—concentration camps

## EAKER, IRA C.
22-4　　　　　　　　　　Failure of Allies to bomb Auschwitz

## FLANNER-SOLANO
17　　　　　　　　　　　"Report on the Concentration Camp at Buchenwald" (1945)

## GERMAN CAPTURED DOCUMENTS
403　　　　　　　　　　Concentration camp matters
f. 67

404　　　　　　　　　　Resettlement and extermination of Jews
f. 94

408　　　　　　　　　　Transportation and extermination of Jews
f. 126

409　　　　　　　　　　Use of concentration camp inmates for manufacturing
f. 145

## MC CRIGHT, EWELL R.
　　　　　　　　　　　　Casualty and prisoner records of American and other soldiers, with observations of atrocities at Buchenwald and Auschwitz

## NICHOLS, WILLIAM I.
8　　　　　　　　　　　Eisenhower Atrocity Trip—
　　　　　　　　　　　　　Buchenwald—photos, camp hospital records, 1945
　　　　　　　　　　　　　Dachau—briefings, photos, captured correspondence, 1945

## *PATTON, GEORGE S. JR.
115　　　　　　　　　　Photographs of liberated concentration camps (1945)
39　　　　　　　　　　　De-Nazification (1945)

## REMARQUE, ERICH MARIE
　　　　　　　　　　　　Spark of Life—manuscript copies of book pertaining to concentration camps

*The Jewish Experience*

**SPAATZ, CARL**
18-9, 35-7, 139, 143, 182 — Failure of Allies to bomb Auschwitz
83 — Photographs of bombings in Auschwitz area

## b. Eichmann, Adolf

**\*ARENDT, HANNAH**
42-52, 57-60 — Eichmann, Adolf—case and trial

**KLEIN, JULIUS**
Israeli reaction to Eichmann capture

**SELZER, MICHAEL**
Eichmann, Adolf—psychological tests —hospital records

**TAFT, CHARLES P.**
293 — Trial of Eichmann

## c. Hitler, Adolf

**BATCHELDER, JOHN**
5 (item 719) — Autograph (May 3, 1935)

**BORAH, WILLIAM**
515 — Hitler's speech

**DEUEL, WALLACE R.**
Hitler and Germany

## GERMAN CAPTURED DOCUMENTS

310, 409 (f. 148), 410    Hitler, Adolf
(f. 181), 413 (f. 217),
431, 434-35, 437-38,
470-72, 472A-I, 473,
486, 787, 789, 791,
823, 825, 827-28

## HALLGARTEN, GEORGE W. F.
"Adolf Hitler and General Heavy Industry, 1931-1933"

## HITLER, ADOLF
Includes copies of will

## LEWIS, NOLAN DON CARPENTER
Hitler's Nazi flag

## *MEAD, MARGARET
B4, F4    Analysis of Hitler's speech, 1941
I20    "Shall Hitler Call Our Tune?", 1941
M32    Erikson, Erik—clinical analysis of Hitler's imagery

## SCHILLER, JOHANN CHRISTIAN FREDERICH VON
Newsclipping on Hitler's ideology and plan to name Hess as his successor (5/14/1941)

## TOLAND, JOHN
7    Hitler, Adolf

## U.S. LIBRARY OF CONGRESS ARCHIVES
Copyright Records    Copyright application for *Mein Kampf*, Adolf
Miscellany    Hitler (1927)
Box 11

## UNITED STATES WORKS PROGRESS ADMINISTRATION
A999　　　　　　　　　　Radio scripts—"You Can't Do Business with Hitler" by the Office of Emergency Management, undated

## d. Refugees

**ACKERMAN, CARL A.**
124-29　　　　　　　　　Oberlander Trust
　　　　　　　　　　　　　—funds for relocating displaced German scholars and students in the U.S. after the rise of Hitler

**BORAH, WILLIAM E.**
490　　　　　　　　　　Refugees
498　　　　　　　　　　Foreign Affairs: Jewish

**CELLER, EMANUEL**
15, 23　　　　　　　　　Displaced persons' camps (post–WW II)

**\*CORCORAN, THOMAS G.**
　　　　　　　　　　　　Refugees from Nazi Germany

**\*DAVIES, JOSEPH E.**
　　　　　　　　　　　　German refugees

**DODD, WILLIAM E.**
　　　　　　　　　　　　German refugees

**\*FLEXNER, ABRAHAM**
　　　　　　　　　　　　German refugee scholars

**FRANKFURTER, FELIX**
134　　　　　　　　　　Exiled scholars (1932-38)
137　　　　　　　　　　German refugees

**HARRISON, LELAND**
　　　　　　　　　　　　U.S. policy toward and observation of refugees from Nazi-occupied Europe

## HUEBSCH, BENJAMIN

German refugees

## HULL, CORDELL

| | |
|---|---|
| 50 | Myron Taylor's meetings with the Pope (9/42) regarding refugees |
| 59, 66 | Jewish immigration to Palestine |
| 85 | Relief of starving peoples of Europe, 1938-41 |

## ICKES, HAROLD L.

Diaries

Assistance to Dr. Sigmund Freud

Settlement of Jewish refugees in Peru

Requests of Stephen S. Wise, Dr. N. Goldmann, et al., to permit Jewish refugees to settle in Virgin Islands

Dr. Ruth Gruber and Oswego, NY refugee camps

Repercussions of turning refugees away from Palestine

Bergson, Peter (Emergency Conference to Save the Jewish People of Europe), 1943

see also—Henry Wallace Papers, FD Roosevelt Library microfilm

Jews—Emergency Committee to Save the Jewish People of Europe, 1944

## *JACKSON, ROBERT H.

Pre– and post–World War II refugees from Europe

## JELLIFFE, SMITH ELY

Aid to German refugees in the medical profession

## *JESSUP, PHILIP

216    Refugees (1937-43)

## LONG, BRECKINRIDGE

202-04    Relief and refugees (includes Bermuda Conference)

## *MORGENTHAU, HANS J.
                Refugees from Nazi Germany

## NATIONAL COUNCIL OF JEWISH WOMEN—WASHINGTON, D.C. OFFICE
                Refugees, 1940-1949

## *NIEBUHR, REINHOLD
                Rescue of German refugees

## *PATTERSON, ROBERT P.
| | |
|---|---|
| 20-1 | Problems with Jews in post-war refugee camps |
| 169 | Refugee committee |

## ROSENWALD, LESSING J.
| | |
|---|---|
| 2 | Refugee situation in Europe—1939 |
| 5 | German refugee aid and displaced persons |
| 9 | Jewish Labor Committee—East European refugees during and after World War II |
| 49-54 | Refugees—displaced persons of Europe |

## SOBELOFF, SIMON E.
| | |
|---|---|
| 15 | Displaced persons (1947-52) |

## STEINHARDT, LAURENCE A.
| | |
|---|---|
| 45 | War Refugee Board and evacuation of Jews from Europe |

## TAFT, CHARLES P.
                War Relief Control Board

## TAFT, ROBERT A.
| | |
|---|---|
| 586, 967 | Displaced persons (1948) |

## TAYLOR, MYRON
| | |
|---|---|
| Box 1<br>v. 3 (1942)<br>8/11/42 | International refugees, including Jewish world population distribution |

SUBJECTS 139

| | |
|---|---|
| Box 2<br>v. 1 (1943)<br>2/26/43<br>3/1/43 | Stephen S. Wise regarding the deportation of non-Italian Jews from Italy |
| 3/18/43<br>3/22/43 | Transfer of Yugoslav Jews into Poland |
| 6/7/43<br>6/19/43<br>6/25/43<br>7/3/43 | Stephen S. Wise regarding the deportation of Jews in Italy |
| 8/28/43 | Wise and Goldmann visit regarding Jews in territories evacuated by Italian troops |

**TOLAND, JOHN**

Refugees from Nazi-occupied Europe

**WARREN, CHARLES**
8-9     War Relief Control Board

**VEBLEN, OSWALD**
29-33     Refugee file

**VOSKA, EMANUEL V.**

Aid to anti-Nazi German refugees in Czechoslovakia

## e. War Crimes and Trials

**\*ARENDT, HANNAH**
41     Nurnburg War Crimes Trials Seminar (1968)
43     German reaction to Nazi crimes
       Many articles pertaining to Nazi policies

**BIDDLE, GEORGE**

—in 1945 covered Nurnburg trials as journalist and artist

**CELLER, EMANUEL**
14-15 Genocide
235 German war criminals

**CREEL, GEORGE**
6 War criminals

**\*DAVIES, JOSEPH E.**
92-4 War criminals (1943-48)

**HALLGARTEN, GEORGE W. F.**
DeNazification trial of Fritz Thyssen

**HULL, CORDELL**
50 Myron Taylor's meetings with the Pope (9/42) regarding Jewish persecution
59 Jewish persecution (3/20/44)

**\*JACKSON, ROBERT H.**
26 Germans—visitors and requests for aid from Nuremberg citizens, 1948-54
53 "Worst Crime of All"—1945
"The Law Under Which Nazi Organizations are Accused of Being Criminal"—1946
"Some Lessons of the Nuremberg Trial"—1946
54 "Closing Arguments for Conviction of Nazi War Criminals"—1947
"Nuremberg in Retrospect"
93-116 Nuremberg War Crimes Trials
100 Grand Mufti of Jerusalem (Haj Amin El-Husseini)
Nuremberg Trials

**LEWIS, NOLAN DON CARPENTER**
Nurnburg War Crimes Trials

**LONG, BRECKINRIDGE**
212 War criminals (1941-42)

## MC COY, FRANK R.
79                       Military Commission—Trial of Nazi saboteurs, July–August, 1942

## *MEAD, MARGARET
M38                      Jews, 1944-45—studies in national character—includes material regarding the War Crimes Trials

## *MORGENTHAU, HANS J.
                         Opinions on war crimes trials

## NATIONAL COUNCIL OF JEWISH WOMEN—WASHINGTON, D.C. OFFICE
Alpha. files              Genocide
5

## OPPENHEIMER, J. ROBERT
76                       War crimes trials

## PULITZER, JOSEPH II
74                       Nurnburg Trials, 1945-1946
97-99                    Nazi war crimes, 1941-1946

## *RIBICOFF, ABRAHAM A.
571                      Nazis, alleged and hunters

## TAFT, ROBERT A.
628-30, 862, 877, 909     Nurnburg trials

## TAYLOR, MYRON
Box 1                   Execution of 200,000 Jews
v. 3 (1942)
p. 27–9/42

Box 2                   Henry Morgenthau, Jr., and Pope's interest in persecution of European Jewry
v. 1 (1943)
5/15/43

Box 5A  German atrocities (copy in box 1, supplement
v. 2 (1940-45)  p. 14)
Pt. I
10/20/42
8/23/44   Winston Churchill on the punishment of war criminals

Pt. II   Persecution of Jews by Nazis
9/22/42
p. 12, 20

**TOLAND, JOHN**
30   Nurnburg War Crimes Trials—photographs

**WASHINGTON, GEORGE THEODORE**
   War crimes trials

## f. Warsaw Ghetto

**CELLER, EMANUEL**
364   Warsaw Ghetto uprising

**DAVIDSON, JO**
14   Warsaw Memorial

**TYLOR, MYRON**
Box 1   Jews in Poland—Warsaw Ghetto
v. 3 (1942)
p. 125-6: 9/26/42
p. 127: 10/21/42

## g. Miscellany

**AMERICAN PSYCHOLOGICAL ASSOCIATION**
H4   Jewish psychologists in Germany (1933)

## *ARENDT, HANNAH
1                           Restitution
62                        Nazism

## BORAH, WILLIAM E.
478, 521                Nazis

## CARR, WILBUR J.
American relations with Nazi Germany, 1933-1939

## CATT, CARRIE CHAPMAN
10                        "Nazis and Nazism," March 30, 1938

## CLAPPER, RAYMOND
135-41               Germany (1934-41)
160                      Jews (1939)

## DAVIS, ELMER
1                           Pleas for aid to escape from Nazi-occupied Poland (1944)

## DODD, WILLIAM E.
40-50                Correspondence while ambassador to Germany (1933-37)
40                       Hess, Rudolph

## FITZPATRICK, JAMES M.
Collection of Alfred Rosenberg correspondence, 1936-45

## *JACKSON, ROBERT H.
110                      Bormann, Martin
112                      Goebbels' diary

## *EINSTEIN, ALBERT
Plight of Jews in Nazi Germany

## FRANKFURTER, FELIX
| | |
|---|---|
| 137-38 | Germany and refugees |
| 126, 137-38, 159 | Nazism |

## FRIEDENWALD, HARRY
Treatment of Jews in Nazi Germany—1933

## FURMAN, BESS
47     Nazi propaganda

## GERMAN CAPTURED DOCUMENTS
| | |
|---|---|
| 249 | Lists of Jews from Stuttgart |
| 409 (f. 149) | Jews among Volksdeutsche |
| 678-82 | Institut zur Enforschung der Judenfrage |
| 748-67 | List of Nazi party members outside of Germany |
| 154, 772 | Dr. Karl Stumpp |
| 309 | Martin Bormann |
| | Albert Speer |
| 389-419 | Heinrich Himmler |
| 399, 435, 790 | Joseph Goebbels |
| 566-68 | Herman Goering |
| 790 | Rudoph Hess |
| | Julius Streicher |

## GOW, JAMES AND D'USSEAU, ARNAUD
Playscripts of *Tomorrow the World* (1942-43)

## *HENDERSON, LOY W.
20     Memoirs, 1938-42—include many references to Hitler and Germany

## HOWARD, ROY
Jews in Germany, 1930's
   —includes Kristallnacht

## HULL, CORDELL
58     Criticism of the Nazi regime

## ICKES, HAROLD L.
Diaries — Hitler's treatment of Jews
Nazi propaganda
Joseph Goebbels
Herman Goering

## LEWIS, NOLAN D.C.
4 — *Some Psychological Hypotheses on Nazi Germany*
5 — Case studies—Germany After the War
Rudolf Hess
Nazi Ideology

## LONG, BRECKINRIDGE
161 — Germany (1933)

## *MEAD, MARGARET
B4, M32 — Erikson, Erik—studies on Hitler, Nazis, etc.
G71-6 — Studies of German contemporary culture
M29-34 — Germany—studies in national character
M38 — Jews, 1944-45—includes material on appeals for Jews in Nazi-occupied lands

## MORAL RE–ARMAMENT
255 — Nazism (1933-45)
305-06 — Germany (1933-61)
317 — Jews (1935-43)

## *MORGENTHAU, HANS J.
Nazi Germany

## NATIONAL AMERICAN WOMAN SUFFRAGE ASSOCIATION
91 — "Feminist Reaction to Nazism" (June, 1934)

## *NIEDERLAND, WILLIAM G.
Holocaust victim studies

**PASVOLSKY, LEO**
7                           Nazi Germany and post-war planning

**\*PATTERSON, ROBERT P.**
135                         Germany

**PINCHOT, GIFFORD**
610                         Jews in Germany
748-51                      Hitler's war in Europe

**ROSENWALD, LESSING J.**
1                           Germany, observations of mood, etc.—1936
3, 34                       America First Committee and allegations of Nazi and anti-Semitic viewpoints

**RUSSELL, CHARLES EDWARD**
21 (f. 4057)                Anti-Nazi rallies (1938)

**SELZER, MICHAEL**
                            Herman Goering

**TAYLOR, MYRON**
Box 1                       Jews in unoccupied France
v. 3 (1942)
p. 160—8/31/42
Box 2                       Hungarian Jews
v. 2 (1944-45)
5/24/44
Box 5A
v. 2 (1940-45)
Pt. III
—9/27/44                    Yugoslav Jews
—10/18/44                   Hungarian Jews

**TOLAND, JOHN**
1-32
        *The Last Hundred Days*
          —fall of Nazi Germany
          —includes photos of liberated concentration camps

**VON NEUMANN, JOHN**
14         Anti-Nazi meeting of Soviet scientists

**WHITE, JOHN C.**
        U.S. relations with Germany and the rise of Hitler and the Nazi Party

## 3. INQUISITION

**BENSASSON, MAURICE JACQUES**
        1929 letter, in French, relating his family's expulsion from Spain in 1492, its travels to Turkey, and eventually to France. The Sephardic community of Salonica is also referred to.

**CONWAY (GEORGE) TRANSCRIPTS**
        *Jews in Mexico*
          —Inquisition trial of Thomas Trevino de Sobremonte (1642)

**FERGUSSON, DAVID**
        Spanish Inquisition in the Western Hemisphere

**SOLORZANO, PAPELES VARIOS**
        Situation of the Jews in Mexico, 1638-71

## 4. RUSSIAN/SOVIET JEWRY

**BEVERIDGE, ALBERT**

        Kishinev pogrom

**BLAINE, JAMES G.**

        Repression of Russian Jewry

**BORAH, WILLIAM E.**
498, 515, 766-67     Refugees and persecution of Russian Jewry

**BRASOL, BORIS**
5-6, 16, 23-5, 53     Pre-Soviet anti-Semitic activities

**CELLER, EMANUEL**
288, 359-59     Soviet Jews

**COMMONER, BARRY**

        Repression of Soviet Jewry (1970's)

**FISH, HAMILTON**
75, 90, 203     Persecution of Russian Jewry (c. 1870-71)

**FREDERICK, HAROLD**
1     *Persecution of Jews in Russia* (1890)

**\*GARMENT, LEONARD**
5     Soviet Jews, 1973-74

**HARRISON, BURTON N.**
41     Resolution requesting the President to use his friendly offices in behalf of the Jews in Russia (4/10/1910)

**HAY, JOHN**

        Kishinev pogrom

## KENNAN, GEORGE L.
112                 Pogroms
                     Anti-Jewish activities

## *KISSINGER, HENRY A.
                     Soviet Jews (1973)

## LANSING, ROBERT
                     Persecution of Russian Jewry
                     Participation of Russian Jews in Socialist movement

## MOORE, JOHN BASSETT
93                  Russia and the exclusion of Jews (1913-14)

## *MORGENTHAU, HANS J.
                     Repression of Soviet Jewry

## MORGENTHAU, HENRY SR.
1, 4-5, 9, 18-19, 22    Jewish relief—Russia

## NATIONAL COUNCIL OF JEWISH WOMEN—WASHINGTON, D.C. OFFICE
196                National Conference on Soviet Jewry

## *RIBICOFF, ABRAHAM A.
57, 610            Soviet Jewry (1975-79)
                     —includes reports on Scharansky, Slepak, and Mendelevitch and correspondence from Menachem Begin, Jewish legislators and organizations

## ROOSEVELT, THEODORE
                     Persecution of Russian Jewry

## ROSENWALD, LESSING J.
6                   Russian Jews

**STRAUS, OSCAR S.**

Tsarist repression of Russian Jewry

## 5. MISCELLANY

**\*COHEN, BENJAMIN V.**
2, 5                        Jewish philanthropy

**DANIELS, JOSEPHUS**
524, 677                    Jewish relief (1913-20, 1935-46)

**FISH, HAMILTON**
68, 70, 75, 100             Persecution of Roumanian Jews
80, 87                      Claims of German Jews against Mexico (7/3/1871 and 5/3/1872)

**HARRISON, LELAND**
105                         Jewish activity in Poland

**MORGENTHAU, HENRY SR.**
1, 4-5, 9, 18-9, 22         Jewish relief—Roumania and Turkey
36                          Maltreatment of Jews, 1919

**\*PODHORETZ, NORMAN**
2                           Jerusalem Conference on Terrorism, 1979

**STRAUS, OSCAR S.**

Jewish relief—Roumania, Poland, and Turkey

# Index

Page references for main entries, as defined above on page x, are in **boldface**. All other page references are in ordinary type.

Aaronsohn, Aaron, **19**, 111, 114
Abdul Baha, **107**
Abdullah (king of Jordan), 111
Abraham, Karl, 40
Abzug, Bella S., **19**
Academic Committee on Soviet Jewry, **76**
Ackerman, Carl A., **136**
Ackerman, Carl W., 26, 27, 38, 57, 66, 68, **92, 108**
Actors, 10, 58, 61
Adams Family, 58
Adelman, Kenneth L., **19**
Adler, Alfred, **1, 19**, 40
Adler, Cyrus, **20**
Adler, Felix, **20**
Advertising and public relations, 2, 8, 26
Ahmad Amin, 93
Aiton, George Briggs, 126
Aldrich, Nelson, 42
Algeria, 93, 94, 101, 104, 127
Alinsky, Saul, **20**
Allen, Fred, **124**
Allen, Henry J., 42, 86, **92**
Allen, William A. H., **92, 108**
Alley, T. J., **92**
Allon, Yigal, **20**, 105
Alsop, Joseph and Stewart, 21, 38, 46, 50, 55, 56, **92**
America First Committee, 146
America-Israel Cultural Foundation, **76**, 119
American Christian Palestine Committee, 120

American Council for Judaism, **76**, 115
American Council of Learned Societies, 28, 30, 34, 36, 38, 41, 49, 61, 66, 70, 74, **93–94, 121, 122**
American Emergency Committee for Zionist Affairs, **76**
American Federation of Labor (AFL), 6, 42, 117
American Friends of Hebrew University, **76**
American Friends of the Middle East, **76**
American Friends Service Mission to Palestine, 111
American Fund for Israel Institutions, 120
*American Hebrew*, **85**
*American Hebrew and Jewish Tribune*, 85
American Institute of Aeronautics and Astronautics, 50
American Israel Public Affairs Committee, **76**
American Jewish Alliance, **76**
American Jewish Archives, **74**
American Jewish Committee, **77**
American Jewish Congress, **77**
*American Jewish Congress Digest*, **85**
American Jewish Historical Society, **74**
American Jewish Joint Distribution Committee, **77**
American Jewish League Against Communism, **78**
American Jewish Tercentenary, **78**
American Nazi Party, 129

151

American Palestine Aviation Society, 108
American Palestine Trading Corporation, **78**
American Peace Commission to Versailles, 19, **94, 108, 113**
American Professors for Peace in the Middle East, **78**
American Psychological Association, **142**
*American Scholar,* 28, 34, 37, 50
American Society of Adlerian Psychology, 19
American Society of Landscape Architects, 27
American Zionist Council, **78,** 116
American Zionist Emergency Council, **78**
American Zionist Federation, **78**
Ames, Louise B., 32
Amin, Idi, 119, 131
Anderson, Chandler P., 21
Anderson, Clinton P., 32, 59, **94**
Anglo-American Commission of Inquiry on Palestine, 111
Anglo-American Oil Agreement, 96
Anglo-Palestine Bank, 109
Anglo-Persian Agreement, 101
Anthropologists, 27
Anti-Defamation League, **79,** 130, 131
Anti-Federalists, 87
Anti-Semitism, **128–132,** 146, 148
"Antisemitismus," **128**
Arab-American Oil Company, 101
Arabia, 94. *See also* Saudi Arabia
Arafat, Yasser, 105
Archaeology, 97, 121
Arendt, Hannah, **1, 20,** 33, 43, 45, 46, 47, 53, 54, 55, 64, 75, 76, 78, 79, 80, 82, 85, **94, 113, 124, 128, 132, 134, 139, 143**
Army officers, 8, 9, 11, 33, 46, 55, 60, 63, 65, 71
Arnold, Henry H., 21, 56, **94, 108**
Aron, Willy, 66
Arrhenius, Svante August, 52
Artists, sculptors, and art historians, 11, 13, 17, 26, 32, 64

Asch, Sholem, **21**
Asimov, Isaac, **21**
Assassins, 62
"Asshur Prince of Shomer or Smiles and Tears," 97
Atlantic Union Committee, 77
*Aufbau,* **85**
Auschwitz, 132, 133, 134
Ausubel, Nathan, 90
Authors. *See* Writers

Bacon, Delia S., 35
Baker, Newton D., 21, 51, 54, 82
Baker, Ray Stannard, 21, 28, 38, 42, 51, 57, 68, 70, 71
Bakst, Leon N., **1**
Balderston, John L., 51
Bankers and financiers, 1, 9, 14, 21, 23, 48, 64, 70
Banks, Nathaniel P., 24
Barbados, 131
Barton-Jenifer Families, 24
Baruch, Bernard, **21–23**
Batchelder, John D., 24, 34, 45, 73, **94, 134**
Bayard, Thomas F., 23, 28, 67
Beach, Joseph W., 73
Beale Family, **94**
Beard, David Carter, 48, 71
Beer, George Louis, **1,** 21, **23,** 28, 37, 38, 53, **95, 108**
Begin, Menachem, **23,** 105, 149
Bell, Alexander Graham, 33, **128**
Bellow, Saul, **23**
Belmont, August, **1, 23**
Ben-Gurion, David, **23,** 97, 114, 120
Benjamin, Judah P., **1, 24–26,** 89
Bensasson, Maurice Jacques, **1, 147**
Berenson, Bernard, **26**
Berge, Wendell, 38
Bergson, Peter, **26,** 80, 119, 137
Berkner, Lloyd V., 116
Berlin, Irving, **26**
Berliner, Emile, **2**
Bernays, Edward L., **2, 26–27,** 28, 40, 43, 49, 71, 77, 79, 80, 81, 85, **124**
Bernfeld, Siegfried, **2, 27,** 30, 34, 35, 40, 53, 64, 81

INDEX 153

Bernstein, Leonard, **27**
Bethune, Mary Jane M., 66
Bettelheim, Bruno, **27**
Beveridge, Albert, **148**
Beyer, Otto Sternoff, **2**, 49
Biblical studies, 93, 121–122
Biddle, George, 51, 64, 66, 68, **139**
Biddle, Nicholas, 58
Bigelow, John, **95**
Bingham, June, 55
Bingham, Robert Worth, 21, 28, 55, 56, 57, 59
Black, Hugo L., 28, 30, 31, 37, 38, 40, 47, 65, **124**
Black-Jewish relations, 129, 130, 131, 132
Blackwell Family, 64, 70, **122**
Blaine, James G., **148**
Blair, Francis P., 24
Blair Family, 43
Bliss, Tasker R., **95, 108, 113, 121**
Block, Claude C., 63
Bloom, Sol, **27**
B'nai B'rith, **78**
B'nai B'rith Anti-Defamation League, **79**, 130, 131
B'nai Zion, **79**
Board of Jewish Education (Chicago), 74
Boas, Franz, **27**
Bohr, Niels H. D., **27–28**
Bollingen Foundation, 36, 40, 45, 86
Bonaparte, Charles J., 28
Bonaparte, Marie, 40
Bonsal, Stephen, 21, **95, 128**
Boone, Daniel, **87**
Boorstin, Daniel J., **2**, 28
Borah, William E., 42, 54, **108, 113, 124, 128, 134, 136, 143, 148**
Borglum, John Gutzon, 62
Bormann, Martin, 143, 144
Bornstein, Berta, **2**
Bowen, Catherine Drinker, 38, 64, 69
Brandeis, Louis Dembitz, **2, 28–29,** 88, **113**, 114
Brant, Irving N., **30**, 31, 38, 40, 45, 71
Brasol, Boris, **148**
Brazil, **124**

Breckinridge Family, 71
Breuer, Josef, **2**
Brice, Fanny, **30**
Brill, Abraham, 30, 40
Bristol, Mark L., 46, 59, **95**
Broadcasters, 63
Brotherhood of Sleeping Car Porters, 33, 40, 45, 48, 55, 61, 65, **129**
Browning Family, **95**
Bryan, William Jennings, 21, 32, 75, 84, **121, 129**
Bryson, Lyman L., 75, 79
Buber, Martin, **30**
Buchenwald, 133
Buchwald, Art, **30**
Buck, Solon J., 38, 47, 48, 56, **129**
Bulgaria, 117
Buneau-Varilla, Phillipe, 33
Burton, Harold H., 38
Burwell, William M., 24
Bush, Vannevar, 21, 27, 36, 38, 49, 59, 60, 70
Business executives and merchants, 5, 6, 11, 15, 27, 35, 43, 50, 57, 62, 63, 67, 73
Butler, Benjamin B., 24
Butterfield, Kenyon L., **95**
Buxton, Frank, 114

Cain, James M., 27, 51, 61
Cairns, Huntington, 30, 36, 38, 45, 47, 51, 56, 65
Cameron, Simon, 24
Canica, Jose, 126
Cantor, Eddie, **30**
Cardozo, Benjamin N., **30**
Carnegie, Andrew, 28, 38, 53, 67, 71, **113, 116, 132**
Carpenter, Dudley N., **95**
Carpenter, Frank, 67
Carr, Wilbur J., **143**
Cartoonists, 41
Catt, Carrie Chapman, 64, 68, 82, **124, 143**
Cattell, James McKeen, 20, 27, 34, 36, 42, 62, 67, 68, 71
Causten-Pickett, 24
Celler, Emanuel, **2**, 23, **31**, 33, 35, 37,

40, 44, 47, 49, 53, 54, 55, 58, 59, 60, 65, 70, 71, 75, 76, 77, 78, 79, 80, 81, 82, 83, 84, 85, 86, **96, 108, 113, 117, 129, 124, 136, 140, 142, 148**
Cerf, Bennett, A., **31**
Chaille-Long, Charles, **96**
Chandler, William P., **96**
Chanute, Octave, 50
Chaplains, 88
Charleston, S.C., 91
Chase, Stuart, 34, 49, 61
Cherif Pasha, 99
Chess players, 5
Chestnut, James, 24
Chicago, Ill., 74, 80, 90, 106, 116, 122, 123
*Chicago Jewish Forum*, **85**
Children's Crusade for Children, 48
Churchill, Winston, 142
Ciardi, John, 63, 65
Cincinnati, Ohio, 88
Civil War, 88
Clapp, Verner W., 35
Clapper, Raymond, 21, 38, **125, 129, 143**
Clay, Thomas J., 24
Clemens, Cyril, 70
Cleveland, Grover, 48, 49, 64, 67, 72
Cohan, Jacob, 87
Cohen, Albert Morris, **3**
Cohen, Benjamin V., **3,** 21, 28, **31–32,** 33, 35, 36, 37, 38, 40, 45, 47, 49, 50, 52, 53, 54, 56, 65, 67, 71, 72, 74, 76, 77, 83, 84, 85, **96, 108, 114, 117, 150**
Cohen, Wilbur J., **32**
Colfax, Schuyler, 24
Collectors, 6, 8, 11, 13, 26, 35, 62
Columbus, Ohio, 89
Comedians, 10, 30, 31, 49, 54
*Commentary*, **85**
Commission on Social Action of Reform Judaism, **79**
Committee for Justice and Peace in the Holy Land, 120
Commoner, Barry, **3, 32,** 34, 38, 46, 59, 61, 78, **148**
Communal leaders and activists, 20, 53, 54, 61, 64, 68, 70, 71

Composers. See Musicians, composers, and conductors
Conductors. See Musicians, composers, and conductors
Confederate States of America, 1, 24, 89
Conference on Adult Jewish Education, **79**
Conference on Jewish Philosophy, **79**
Conference on Jewish Social Studies, **79**
Conference on Near Eastern Affairs, **3, 96**
Conference on the Status of Soviet Jews, **79**
Connally, Thomas, **96**
Conrad, Daniel B., **108**
*Contemporary Jewish Record*, **85**
Conway, George, **147**
Coolidge, Calvin, 54, 70
Corcoran, Thomas G., 21, 28, 30, 31, 33, 37, 38, 44, 47, 48, 51, 52, 53, 56, 61, 63, 67, **136**
Corcoran, William W., 23, 24, 38
Cortelyou, George B., 67, 72
Cotton, Charles S., **96**
Cralle, Richard K., 73
Creel, George, 21, **140**
Critics, 45, 69
Crittenden, John J., 24
Croffut, William A., 42, **87**
Crosby, Oscar T., 21, **96**
Culbertson, William S., **96, 114**
Curry, Jabez L. M., 24, 58
Cushing, Caleb, 24
Cutting, Bronson M., 33
Czechoslovakia, 139

Dachau, 133
Dahlgren, John A. B., 24
Daniel Guggenheim Fund, **3**
Daniels, Josephus, 21, 28, 32, 56, 67, **97, 108, 129, 150**
Das, Taraknath, 115
Davidson, Jo, **3, 32,** 66, **117, 142**
Davies, Joseph E., 21, 38, 61, **97, 136, 140**
Davis, Elmer, 60, **129, 143**

Davis, Jefferson, 73
Davis, Norman H., 21
Dayan, Moshe, **32,** 103, 105
Decalogue Society (Organization of Jewish Attorneys in Chicago), **79**
De Hass, Jacob, **32,** 116
Dehaven, Edwin Jesse, **97**
De la Motta, Jacob, **32,** 89
Delano, Columbus, 24
Dembitz, Louis N., 88
Denny, George V., 23, **97**
Derrick, Henry Clay, **97**
Deuel, Wallace R., **134**
De Valera, Eamon, 115
Dickinson, Charles M., **109**
Diplomats, 1, 10,.14, 15, 23, 35, 57, 66, 67
Directors. See Producers and directors
Displaced persons, 105, 136. See also Refugees, Jewish
Disraeli, Benjamin, **3, 32**
Dixon, Frederick, **114**
Dock, Lavinia L., 70, **122**
Dodd, William E., 71, **136, 143**
Douglas, William O., 21, 28, 37, 38, 41, 47, 49, 56, **117**
Doysie, Abel, 54, 74
Dramatists. See Playwrights
Dreikurs, Rudolf, **3,** 19, 56, **117**
Dreyfus, Alfred, **33,** 128
Dropsie College, 123
Dubinsky, David, **33**
Duncan, George Stewart, **97, 121**
Durant, William H., **97**
D'Usseau, Arnaud, **144**

Eaker, Ira C., 26, 68, **97, 109, 133**
Early, Jubal A., 24
Easby-Smith Family, 24
Eban, Abba, **33,** 105, 114
Economists, 2, 4, 6, 9, 14, 16, 36, 41, 66
Edgerton, Henry W., 38
Editors, 31, 47, 52, 58, 65, 69
Educators, 1, 3, 4, 5, 8, 13, 16, 20, 32, 46, 47, 49, 52, 54, 55, 65
Eichmann, Adolf, 134

Einstein, Albert, **4,** 30, **34,** 40, 66, **143**
Einstein, Lewis, **35**
Eisenhower, Dwight, 133
Eisenhower Doctrine, 96
Eizenstat, Stuart E., **35**
Egypt, 92, 93, 94, 95, 96, 97, 98, 100, 101, 102, 103, 104, 105, 106
Elath (Epstein), Eliahu, **35**
El-Husseini, Haj Amin, 100
Eliot, George F., 51
Emergency Conference to Save the Jewish People of Europe, 137
Engineers, 2, 11, 16, 55
Entertainers, 30. See also Actors; Comedians; Singers
ERAmerica, 40, 77, 78, 79, 82, 83
Erikson, Erik H., **35,** 135, 145
Eshkol, Levi, **35**
Ethiopia, 107
Etzioni, Amitai W., **4**
Eustis, George, 24
Evarts (Epstein), Lillian, **4**

Fahy, Charles, 31, 33, 35, 37, 38, 41, 49, 50, 61, 65
Farley, James A., 38
Federation of Jewish Philanthropies, **79**
Federn, Paul, **4,** 26, 27, **35,** 40
Feinberg, Charles E., **4, 35**
Feis, Herbert, **4,** 21, 28, 36, 38, 47, 59, 66, 72, 85, **109, 117**
Feminism, 61, 93, 145
Ferber, Edna, **4, 36**
Fergusson, David, **147**
Feuchtwanger, Lion, **5, 36**
Fillmore, Millard, 24
Fine, Reuben, **5**
Fish, Hamilton, 24, 58, **87, 109, 125, 148, 150**
Fisher, Walter, L., 28
Fiske, Minnie Maddern, 73
Fitzpatrick, James M., **143**
Fitzpatrick, John C., 27, 63
Flanner-Solano, 43, 60, 66, **129, 133**
Fletcher, Henry P., **97**
Flexner, Abraham, **5,** 21, **36,** 37, 48, 62, **136**

Flexner, Bernard, **37**
Force, Peter, **98**
Ford, Henry, 129, 131
Ford Peace Plan, 28, 62, 64, 65
Forney, John W., 24
Fortas, Abe, **37**
Foulke, William Dudley, 20, 42, **98**
France, 128, 146, 147
Frankfurter, Felix, **5**, 19, 20, 21, 23, 27, 28, 30, 31, 33, 34, 36, 37, **38–39**, 42, 44, 47, 48, 50, 51, 52, 53, 54, 55, 56, 57, 58, 59, 62, 63, 64, 65, 68, 70, 71, **109**, **114**, **117**, **129**, 130, **136**, **144**
Frankfurter Zionist Collection, 19, 28, 32, 38, 47, 51, 53, 71
Franklin, Benjamin, 63, **87**
Frederick, Harold, **148**
French, Daniel Chester, 56
French Papers Claims, 89
Freud, Anna, **5**, **40**
Freud, Harry, **5**, 40
Freud, Sigmund, **5**, 26, 27, 34, 35, **40**, 70, 73, 86, 137
Frey, John P., **121**
Frey, Joseph P., 33, 41, 42, 44, 50
Friedenwald, Harry, **5**, **144**
Friedman, Harry T., **87**
Fuller, Melville W., 67
Furman, Bess, 48, 61, 78, **123**, **144**


Gamow, Barbara and George, 21, 28, 34, 69
Gandhi, Mohandas, 115
Garfield, Harry A., 21
Garfield, James A., 24, 63
Garfield, James R., 72
Garment, Leonard, **5**, 54, 60, **98**, **117**, **125**, **129**, **148**
Gaza Strip, 111
German Captured Documents, 66, **133**, **135**, **144**
Germany, 88, 125, 128, 130, 134–146. See also West Germany
Gertz, Elmer, **6**, 74, 76, 77, 79, 85
Ghent, William J., 51
Gilcrest, Huntington, 36, 51, **98**, **109**

Gilder, Helene de Kay, 48
Ginsberg, Allen, **40**
Ginsburg, Ruth Bader, **40**
Gitelson, Maxwell, **6**, 27, **117**
Glasman, B., 91
Gleason, Arthur H., 38, 47, 49, 51, 53, 71, **125**
Goebbels, Joseph, 143, 144, 145
Goering, Herman, 144, 145, 146
Goldberg, Arthur J., **40–41**
Goldberg, Rube, **41**
Goldenweiser, Emanuel A., **6**, 29, **41**, 109
Goldman, Emma, **41**
Goldmann, Nachum, **42**, 137, 139
Goldmark, Pauline D., **6**, 29, **42**
Goldsborough, Louis M., **6**
Gompers, Samuel, **6**, **42**
Goodwin, James H., 24
Gordon, Ruth, 26, 36, 38, 46, 54
Gosnell, Harold, **98**
Goudsmit, Samuel Abraham, **6**
Government officials, 1, 2, 3, 5, 8, 9, 10, 12, 13, 14, 19, 20, 21, 24, 27, 28, 31, 32, 35, 45, 46, 47, 48, 49, 50, 52, 55, 56, 57, 58, 59, 60, 61, 63, 64, 67, 70, 71, 73. See also Diplomats
Gow, James, **144**
Graham, Fred, 37
Grand Island, N.Y., 87
Granik, Theodore, 31, 45, 63, 83, **109**
Grant, Ulysses S., 63
Gratz, Benjamin, **6**, **43**
Gratz, Rebecca, **7**, **43**
Great Britain, 88, 109, 110
Green, Duff, 58
Green, Theodore Francis, **98**
Gregory, Thomas Watt, 21, 28
Gresham, Walter Q., 67
Griswold, Ralph E., **98**
Gruber, Ruth, 137
Gruenberg, Benjamin C. and Sidonie M., **7**, 43
Gruenberg, Sidonie M., **43**
Guggenheim, Harry F., **7**
Guiterman, Arthur, **7**
Gwinn, William N., 24

Habima Theatre, **80**
Hackworth, Green H., 5, **98, 117**
Hadassah, **80,** 115
Hagedorn, Hermann, 21
Haifa, University of, **75**
Haig, Alexander, **98**
Hale, George E., 34
Hallgarten, George W. F., **135, 140**
Halsey, William F., 45, 46, 56, 68, 76, 81
Hamburg, Germany, 88
Hamlin, Charles S., 21, 29
Hammond, James H., 24
Harbord, James G., **98**
Harding, Warren G., **99**
Harris, Isham G., 24
Harris, William Torrey, **99**
Harrison, Benjamin, 33, 67
Harrison, Burton N., 24, **148**
Harrison, Florence J., 21, 26, 34, 84
Harrison, Gilbert A., 23, 38, 41, 43, 45, 51, 60, 61, 62, 66
Harrison, Leland, **99, 136, 150**
Hay, John, 26, 72, **148**
Hayes, Isaac Israel, **7**
Hebrew-American Democratic Club (New Haven, Conn.), 87
Hebrew Committee of National Liberation, **80**
Hebrew language, 91
Hebrew Union College–Jewish Institute of Religion, **74,** 115, 123
Hebrew University, **74**
Hebrew University Hospital, **75**
Hecht, Anthony, **43**
Hecht, Ben, **7, 43**
Heifetz, Jascha, **43**
Heine, Heinrich, **43**
Hellman, Lillian, **7, 43**
Henderson, Loy W., 35, 42, 56, 62, 65, 71, **99, 109, 114, 144**
Hertz, Emanuel, **7,** 71, **88,** 89
Hertzberg, Arthur, **44**
Herzl, Theodor, **44,** 113, 115
Hess, Rudolf, 143, 144, 145
Hillel Foundation, **80**
Hillman, Sidney, **44**

Himmler, Heinrich, 144
Hines, Lewis G., **117**
Hirsch, Maurice de, **44**
Hirschmann, Ira A., **44**
Historians, 1, 2, 10, 23, 28, 30, 36, 46, 52, 54, 69
Hitler, Adolf, **134–135,** 144, 147
Holmes, George F., 24
Holmes, John Haynes, 29, 30, 38, 41, 45, 48, 53, 71, 73, 79, 81, 82, 83, 86, **114,** 115, **125, 130**
Holmes, Oliver Wendell, Jr., 35
Holocaust, **132–147**
Holt, Joseph, 24
Hooper, Stanford C., 63, **99**
Hostovsky, Egon, **7**
Hotchkiss, Jedediah, 24
Hotze, Henry, 24
Houdini, Harry, **45**
Howard, Roy, 21, 36, 59, 69, 71, **99, 109, 130, 144**
Howe, Irving, **45**
Huddy, Joshua, 88, 90
Huebsch, Benjamin W., **8,** 21, 29, 34, 36, 38, 41, 43, **45,** 47, 48, 49, 51, 52, 53, 64, 71, 72, 73, 74, 76, 77, 81, **130, 137**
Hughes, Charles Evans, 34, 54, 67, **99**
Hull, Cordell, 21, **99, 109, 137, 140, 144**
Hungary, 146
Hurst, Fannie, **45**
Husein Pasha, 94
Hussein (king of Jordan), 105
Hutchison, Ralph Waldo, **99**

Ickes, Harold L., 22, 26, 27, 29, 30, 31, 33, 34, 36, 37, 38, 40, 42, 44, 47, 48, 50, 51, 53, 55, 56, 57, 62, 65, 68, 71, 79, 80, 81, 86, **100, 110, 114, 118, 125, 130, 137, 145**
Ilg, Frances G., 32
Immigration, 88
India, 124
Indian languages, 91, **126**
Inman, Samuel Guy, **100, 118**

Inquisition, **147**
Institute of Jewish Affairs, **75,** 89
Institut zur Enforschung der Judenfrage, 144
Inter-Parliamentary Union, **100, 118**
Inventors, 2, 9, 50
Iran, 92, 93, 94, 96, 99, 100, 101, 102, 103, 107. See also Persia
Iraq, 96, 99, 100, 101, 102, 103
Isaacs, Myer W., 88
Isakower, Otto, **8**
Islam, 93, 102
Israel, State of, 98, 101, 105, 108, 116–120, 134
Israel Bonds, 117, 118
Israeli Air Force Technical School, 117
Israeli Ambassador's Ball, 117
Israeli officials and public figures, 19, 20, 23, 26, 30, 32, 33, 35, 47, 53, 54, 60, 64, 65, 70, 71
*Israel Magazine,* **85**
Israel Philharmonic Orchestra, 117
Ives, Frederic and Herbert, 34
Izat Bey, 106

Jackson, Andrew, 55
Jackson, Robert H., 22, 29, 30, 31, 38, 65, **100, 130, 137, 140, 143**
Jackson, Shirley, 31, 54, 69
James, Marquis, 22
Jameson, J. Franklin, 23, 74
Jardine, William M., **100**
Javits, Jacob, **45–46**
Jefferson, Thomas, 32, 58, 89
Jelliffe, Smith Ely, 40, **137**
Jerusalem, 106, 108, 109, 111, 117, 118, 121, 122
Jerusalem Conference on Terrorism, 150
Jessup, Philip C., 39, **100, 137**
Jewish Agricultural Society, **80,** 113
Jewish Chautauqua Society, **80**
*Jewish Chronicle,* **86**
*Jewish Comment,* **86**
Jewish Community Center, **75**
Jewish Community Council of Chicago, **80**
Jewish Community Councils, **80**
Jewish Cultural Reconstruction, **80**
*Jewish Daily Courier,* **86**
*Jewish Daily News,* **86**
Jewish Foster Home (Washington, D.C.), 90
Jewish Labor Committee, **80,** 138
*Jewish Life,* **86**
Jewish Mental Health Society, **81**
Jewish Ministers' Association, **81**
*Jewish Morning Journal,* **86**
Jewish National Fund, **81**
Jewish National Workers Alliance of America, **81**
*Jewish Newsletter,* **86**
Jewish Organizations, Miscellaneous, **82**
Jewish Palestine Appeal, **81**
Jewish Philanthropies, **81**
Jewish Publication Society, **81**
*Jewish Symbols,* **86**
*Jewish Tribune,* **86**
Jewish Theological Institute, **75**
Jewish Theological Seminary of America, **75**
Jewish War Veterans of the United States, **81**
Jewish Welfare Board, **81**
*Jewish Year Book,* **86**
Jewish Youth Movement and School Reform, **81**
Jews, ethnic, characterological, and miscellaneous studies, 89, 90–91, 118, 124–127
Johnson, Nelson T., 56
Johnson, Reverdy, 24, 32
Johnston, Albert S., 24
Johnston, Mercer C., 39, 71
Johnston, William P., 25
Jones, Jesse H., 22
Jordan, 101, 102, 106. See also Trans-Jordan
Joshua (biblical leader), 121
Journalists, 9, 11, 30, 46, 50, 55, 60, 65, 66
Judah, Henry Moses, **8**
Judah Magnes Foundation, **82**

Judaism, 121, 123. See also Biblical studies
Judges. See Lawyers and jurists

Kagan, Solomon Robert, **8**
Kanin, Garson, **8**, 39, **118**
Katz, Joseph, **8**
Kaufman, George Simon, **8**, 36, **46**
Kellock, Katherine A., 45
Kellogg, Frank B., 51
Kennan, George L., 71, **110, 125, 149**
Kennedy, Joseph, 130
Kilmer, Alfred Joyce, 69
King, Ernest J., 22, 51, 56, 68
King, Judson, 50
King-Crane Commission, 102
Kingsbury, John A., 29, 34, 36, 48, 51, 56, 57, 67, 70, 71
Kishinev, 148
Kissinger, Henry A., **8**, 32, **46**, 55, 56, 60, **101, 149**
Klein, Julius, **9**, 23, 45, **46, 118, 134**
Kleine, George, 27
Knox, Dudley W., 31
Knox, Franklin, 39, 51
Koch, Edward I., **47**
Kolleck, Teddy, **47**
Kook, Hillel. See Bergson, Peter
Korda, Alexander, **47**
Kraus, Hans P., **9**
Kraus, Karl, **9**
Kristol, Irving, **47**
Kroll, Jack, **9**, 41, 44
Krug, Julius A., 22, 50
Krutch, Joseph Wood, 59, 69
Kubie, Lawrence S., **9**
Kuwait, 101

Labor leaders, 2, 6, 9, 12, 33, 42
La Follette Family, 29, 32, 39, 42, 44, 45, 47, 50, 51, 70, **110**
Land, Emory Scott, 22
Landis, James M., 29, 30, 39, 50, 56, **101**
Lane, Gertrude, 36

Langmuir, Irving, **9**, 28
Lansing, Robert L., 29, 42, 53, 54, 57, 62, 64, 67, **101, 110, 149**
Laski, Harold J., **9**, 47–48
Lawrence, T. E. (Lawrence of Arabia), 95
Lawrie, Lee, 48, 63
Lawyers and jurists, 2, 3, 5, 6, 7, 10, 12, 14, 16, 28, 30, 31, 32, 35, 36, 37, 40, 45, 47, 49, 50, 52, 53, 54, 55, 58, 60, 61, 65, 66, 67, 68, 72
Lazarus, Emma, **48**
Leadership Conference on Civil Rights, **130**
Leahy, William D., **102, 110**
Lear, Tobias, **101**
Lebanon, 92, 95, 96, 101, 102, 104, 107
Lee, Samuel P., 25
Leffingwell, Russell C., 22
Lehman, Hebert H., **9**, 48
Leinsdorf, Erich, **49**
Leland, Waldo G., 39
Lerner, Abba Ptachya, **9**
Leventhal, Harold, **10**, **49**
Levi, Edward H., **49**
Levy, Jacob C., 122
Levy, Jefferson M., **49**, 89
Levy, Uriah Phillips, **10**
Lewis, Jerry, **49**
Lewis, Nolan Don Carpenter, **135, 140, 145**
Lewisohn, Ludwig, **49**
Libby, Frederick J., **110**
Libro de Judio, 126
Libya, 93, 95, 101, 102, 103, 104
Lilienthal, David E., **49–50**
Lilienthal, Otto, **50**
Lincoln, Abraham, 87, **88**, 89
Lindbergh, Charles, 130
Lindsey, Benjamin Barr, 20, 29, 37, 51, 53, 57, 64, 67, 71
Linowitz, Sol M., **50**
Lipmann, Fritz Albert, **10**
Lippincott, Richard, **88**, 90
Lippman, Walter, **50–52**
Lipset, Seymour M., **52**
Lipsky, Louis, **52**

160    *The Jewish Experience*

Loeb, Jacques, **10,** 26, 34, 36, 40, **52,** 53
London Exhibition of 1851, 25
Long, Breckinridge, 22, 33, 56, 71, **110, 130, 137, 140, 145**
Lorand, Sandor, 40
Louchheim, Katie S., 31, 72, 74
Lovell, Mansfield, 25
Lowenthal, Max, **52**
Lower, Abraham, Jr., 88
Luce, Clair Boothe, 22, 84, **101, 115**
Luce, Henry R., 22, 46, 76, 84
Ludwig, Emil, **10,** 52
Lynd, Robert S. and Helen M., 20, 35, 52

McAdoo, William G., 29, 64
McCook Family, 25
McCormick, Lynde D., 22
McCoy, Frank R., 39, **141**
McCright, Ewell R., **133**
McGee, William J., 27
McGowen, Samuel, 22
McGranery, James P., 61
Mack, Julian, **53**
McKinley, William, 59, 64, 67, 72
McLean, Evalyn Walsh, 22, 27, 30, 56
MacLeish, Archibald, 22, 26, 27, 29, 31, 36, 39, 43, 44, 46, 48, 49, 50, 51, 54, 56, 59, 62, 68, 69, 72
McPherson Family, 25
McVay, Charles B., Jr., **121**
MacVeagh, Franklin, **102**
Madison, James, 32, 58, **89**
Madol, Hans R. (Gerhard Salomon), **10**
Magicians, 45
Magnes, Judah L., **53,** 116, 132
Mailer, Norman, **53**
Maimonides Institute, **82**
Malamud, Bernard, **10, 54**
Malik, Charles H., 51, **102, 110, 118**
Malina, Frank J., 28, 44
Mallory, Stephen R., 25
Mangum, Willie P., 25
Mann, Arthur W., 31
Marble, Manton M., 23
Marcus, Jacob R., **54**
Marcy, William L., 23, 25, 58

Marshall, Charles C., 51
Marshall, Louis, **54**
Martin, Letitia B., 25
Marx, Groucho, **10,** 49, 60
Marx, Harpo, **54**
Marx, Karl, **10, 54**
Mason, Alexander Macomb, **102**
Mason, James M., 25
Materials for Israel, Inc., 120
Mathematicians, 16, 70
Mathews, F. David, 46
Mauldin, William, 30
Maury, Matthew F., 25
Maxwell, Perriton, 45
Mead, Margaret, 19, 26, 27, 28, 32, 33, 35, 40, 41, 43, 46, 51, 53, 60, 62, 63, 69, 75, 77, **89, 102, 110, 118, 135, 141, 145**
Mearns, David A., 61, 78
Medicine Maya—Libro de Judio de Solola, 126
Meier, Nellie Simmons, **11,** 43
Meir, Golda, **54,** 105
Mendelevitch, Iosif, 149
Mendelssohn, Felix, 122
Merchants. *See* Business executives and merchants
Merriam, C. Hart, **118**
Mervine, Thomas, **123**
Mexico, 126, 147, 150
Meyer, Agnes, 20, 29, 35, 41, 51, 68, 74, 75, 78, 80, **118, 125**
Meyer, Eugene, **11,** 22, 26, 27, 29, 30, 31, 39, 41, 44, 48, 51, 53, **55,** 56, 62, 66, 67, 68, 75, 77, 78, 80, 82, 84, 85, **119, 125**
Michener, James, 55, **122**
Middle East Industries, Inc., 119
Middle East Oil Company, 101
Middleton, George, 27, 29, 36, 37, 39, 41, 43, 45, 46, 47, 50, 51, 58, 59, 61, 66, 68, 70, 72, 73
Mies van der Rohe, Ludwig, 41
Mikva, Abner J., **55**
Miller, Arthur, **55**
Mills, Ogden L., 22, 55, 65
Milton, George F., 25, 50

INDEX 161

Mizrachi Organization of America, **82**
Mizrachi Women of New York, **82**
Monroe, James, 58
Montgomery Family, 55, **102**
Moore, John Bassett, 33, 67, **115, 119, 125, 149**
Moore, Merrill, 31, 43, 51, 69
Moral Re-Armament, 55, **102, 145**
Moran, Benjamin, 25
Mordecai, Alfred, **11,** 43, **55**
Morgenthau, Hans J., 20, 26, 28, 32, 34, 39, 46, 47, 49, 51, **55–56,** 57, 59, 62, 64, 68, 74, 75, 76, 77, 78, 79, 80, 85, 86, **103, 110, 115, 119, 125, 138, 141, 145, 149**
Morgenthau, Henry Jr., **11, 56–57,** 141
Morgenthau, Henry M., Sr., **11,** 20, 22, 29, 34, 45, 52, 54, 56, **57,** 64, 67, 70, 72, 73, **89, 103, 111, 115, 149, 150**
Morgenthau, Henry, 19
Morocco, 87, 97, 100, 101, 102, 107
Morris, Robert, 63
Moseley, George van Horn, **130,** 132
Moses (biblical leader), 121
Moses, Raphael Jacob, **11**
Moses, Robert, **58**
Moulton, Louise Chandler, 73
Mount, Charles M., **11**
Mowrer, Edgar A., 33, 35, 45, 58
Mowrer, Edgar and Lillian, 22, 26, 50, 51, 55, 61, 63
Moynihan, Daniel Patrick, **103**
Muhammed, 93
Muni, Paul, **58**
Murdock, Victor, 22, 29, 42, 56
Murphree, Egar V., 69
Musicians, composers, and conductors, 26, 27, 43, 49, 66
Myer, Albert J., 25

Nahon (U.S. vice-consul in Morocco), 87
Nasser, Gamal, 97
National American Woman Suffrage Association, 64, **145**
National Association for the Advancement of Colored People (NAACP), 29, 34, 39, 66, 72, 77, 78, 79, 80, 81, 82, 83, 86, **126, 131**
National Board for Historical Service, **126**
National Civic Federation, 44, 54, 57, 67, **115, 131**
National Conference of Christians and Jews, **82**
National Conference on Soviet Jewry, **82,** 149
National Consumers League, 42, 82
National Council of Jewish Women, **11, 82–83**
National Council of Jewish Women—Washington Office, **12,** 77, 78, 79, 82, 83, 84, 85, **103, 111, 115, 119, 126, 131, 138, 141, 149**
National Federation of Temple Brotherhoods, **83**
National Federation of Temple Sisterhoods, **83**
National Jewish Women's Organizations, **83**
National Ladies Auxiliary of Jewish War Veterans of the U.S.A., **83**
National Urban League, **131**
National Woman's Party, 31, 33, 39, 41, 44, 45, 48, 61, 64, 83
National Women's Trade Union League of America, 42
Naval officers, 3, 6, 10, 15, 61
Nazis, Nazism, 129, 133, 134–135, 140, 143, 144, 147
Near East Relief, 92, 99, 103, 106, 108
Neufeld, Maurice F., **12**
Neumann, Emanuel, **58**
Newcomb, Simon, 27
New Haven, Conn., 87
New York City, 88, 90, 91
Nichols, William I., 26, 30, 31, 41, 50, 58, 61, **133**
Niebuhr, Reinhold, 39, 46, 48, 56, 72, **103, 111, 138**
Niederland, William G., **12, 145**
Nielson, Frederick K., 22, 53, **103**
Nizer, Louis, **58**
Noah, Mordecai Manuel, **58,** 87, 89

North, Simon N. D., 25

Oberammergau Passion Play, 128
Oberlander Trust, 136
Ochs, Adolph S., **59**
Odets, Clifford, **12, 59**
Ogilvy, David, 26, 58, 81
O'Laughlin, John C., 63, 67
Olney, Richard, 42
Oman, 101
Oppenheimer J. Robert, **12,** 22, 28, 32, 34, 36, 37, 39, 46, 48, 50, 51, 56, **59,** 60, 61, 68, 69, 70, 71, 74, 75, 77, 80, 82, 84, **103, 119, 141**
Orr, William, **111**
ORT Federations, **83**
Osborn, Fairfield, 22, 51, 55
Osborne, John, **103**
Oscar S. Straus Memorial Association, 67
Oswego, N.Y., 137
Overholser, Winfred, 22
Owings, Nathaniel, 41
Oxnam, G. Bromley, 50

Palestine, 92, 94, 95, 98, 100, 105, **107–113,** 114, 115, 137. See also Israel, State of
Palestine Economic Corporation, 111
Palestine Endowment Fund, **83**
Palestine Foundation Fund, **83,** 109
Palestine Liberation Organization (PLO), 101
Palestine Partition Resolution, **15, 120**
Palestine Restoration Fund, 113
Parker, Dorothy, **59–60**
Parsons, William S., 22, 50
Pasvolsky, Leo, **111, 146**
Patterson, Daniel Todd, **103**
Patterson, Robert P., 22, 30, 31, 33, 39, 46, 48, 50, 52, 53, 56, 58, 62, **111, 138, 146**
Patton, George S., Jr., 48, **104, 133**
Pecquet, du Bellet Paul, 25
Perelman, S. J., **60**
Peres, Shimon, **60,** 105
Perlmutter, Nathan, **60,** 104
Pershing, John J., 22

Persia, 94, 95, 99, 105. See also Iran
Pertschuk, Michael, **12**
Peru, 137
Philadelphia, 91
Philadelphia Hebrew Congregation, 88
Philanthropists, 6, 7, 15, 21, 43, 62, 64, 70
Phillips, Philip, 25, 89
Phillips, Philip Family, **12, 122**
Philosophers, 1, 10, 20, 30, 54, 66
Physicians, 2, 7, 8, 9, 32, 43, 59
Piccard Family, 34
Pickens-Bonham, 25
Pickett, John T., 25
Pierce, Franklin, 25
Pinchot, Amos, 29, 41, 48, 52, 70, **104**
Pinchot, Cornelia, 37
Pinchot, Gifford, 29, **146**
Pincus, Gregory, **13**
Pinfold, Charles, **131**
Pittman, Kay, 22, 57
Playwrights, 7, 8, 12, 43, 46, 55, 58, 59
Podhoretz, Norman, **13,** 19, 20, 23, 33, 40, 43, 44, 46, 47, 53, 60, 62, 65, 66, 69, 77, 79, 84, 85, **104, 119, 126, 131, 150**
Poets, 4, 7, 14, 15, 40, 43, 48, 59, 63, 65, 69
Poland, 139, 143, 150
Political scientists, 1, 9, 11, 14, 20, 47, 55, 62, 64
Pool, David de Sola, **60**
Porter, David Dixon, **89, 104**
Portuguese Manuscripts, **126**
Preble, Edward, **104**
Pritchett, Henry S., 113
Producers and directors, 8, 14, 47, 49, 66
Pro-Palestine Federation, **83**
*Pro-Palestine Herald*, **86,** 114
Psychologists, Psychiatrists, and Psychoanalysts, 1, 2, 3, 4, 5, 6, 8, 9, 12, 13, 19, 27, 35, 40
Publishers, 8, 9, 13, 14, 31, 42, 45, 46, 59, 60, 63, 66, 68
Pulitzer, Joseph I, **13, 60,** 69
Pulitzer, Joseph II, 22, 26, 27, 50, 52, 55, 59, 60, 68, 72, **141**

# INDEX

Putnam, Frederick W., **89**

Rabbinical Assembly of America, **83**
Rabi, Isidore I., **60**
Rabin, Yitzchak, **60**
Rahv, Philip, 85
Randall, James G., **89**
Randolph, A. Philip, **119, 131**
Rapaport, David, **13,** 27, **119, 132**
Rayner, Isidore, **60**
Redfield, William C., 29
Redfield Family, 42
Refugees
  Arab, 96, 97
  East European, 89
  Jewish, 111, **136–139,** 144, 148
  Syrian, 102
Reid Family, 22, 23, 26, 27, 30, 31, 33, 34, 35, 36, 37, 39, 42, 44, 46, 47, 49, 50, 52, 55, 57, 58, 59, 62, 63, 64, 65, 66, 67, 70, 71, 72, 77, **119**
Religious leaders, 53, 71
Remarque, Erich Marie, **133**
Revolutionaries, Russian, 69
Revolutionary War, 63
Reynolds, Thomas C., 25
Ribicoff, Abraham A., **13,** 23, 32, **61, 89, 104, 111, 119, 141, 149**
Richberg, Donald R., 29, 39, 50
Rickover, Hyman G., **61**
Riis, Jacob, **126**
Rives, William C., 25
Roberts, Edmund, **104**
Robinson, Edward G., **61**
Rogge, Oetje John, 61
Roman, Alfred, 25
Roosevelt, Kermit, 27, 45, 46, 52, 57, 58, 68, 72, **104**
Roosevelt, Theodore, 20, 22, 29, 39, 42, 48, 52, 54, 57, 59, 60, 63, 64, 67, 68, 70, 72, 73, **126,** 130, **149**
Roosevelt, Theodore, Jr., 22, 26, 36, 39, 42, 52, 54
Root, Elihu, 67
Rose, Ernestine L. S. P., **61**
Rosenberg, Alfred, 143
Rosenberg, Ethel and Julius, **61**

Rosenman, Samuel I., **61–62**
Rosenthal, Albert, **13**
Rosenwald, Lessing Julius, **13,** 19, 20, 30, 33, 37, 39, 49, 50, 53, 57, 58, 59, **62,** 68, 74, 75, 77, 79, 84, 86, **89, 104, 111, 115, 119–120, 123, 126, 132, 138, 146, 149**
Rosten, Leo C., **62**
Roth, Philip, **13, 62**
Rothschild, Meyer Amschel, **14**
Roumania, 150
Ruby, Jack, **62**
Rudolph, Curo H., **90**
Rukeyser, Muriel, **14, 63**
Russell, Bertrand, 103
Russell, Charles Edward, 22, 34, 45, 63, 72, **112, 115, 123, 127, 132, 146**
Russian/Soviet Jewry, **148–150**
Russian Orthodox Greek Catholic Church in Alaska, **112**
Rutledge, Wiley B., 30

Sacco-Vanzetti Case, 39
Sadat, Anwar, 103, 105
Salomon, Edward Selig, **63**
Salomon, Haym, **63**
Salonica, 147
Sanders, George N., 25
Sanger, Margaret, 31, 41, 44, 45, 57, 78, 80, 83, **105, 112, 123**
Saphirstein, Jacob, **63**
Sarnoff, David, **63**
Saudi Arabia, 102
Savannah, Ga., 89
Sayre, Francis B., 49, **105, 112**
Scharansky, Anatoly, 149
Schiff, Jacob, **64**
Schiller, Johann Christian Frederich von, **121, 135**
Scholem, Gershom Gerhard, **64**
Schoolcraft, Henry Rowe, 25, 58
Schurz, Carl, 59, 67
Schuyler, Eugene, **105**
Schwellenbach, Lewis, 36, 57
Schwimmer, Rosika, **14, 64**
Scientists, 3, 4, 6, 9, 10, 12, 13, 15, 16, 21, 27, 32, 34, 52, 59, 60, 68, 69, 70, 147

Scott, Charles L., **105**
Selfridge, Thomas O., 25
Selzer, Michael I., **14, 64, 134, 146**
Serouya, Henri, 66
Shahn, Ben, **64**
Shapiro, Karl Jay, **4, 14,** 35, 53, 54, 55, **65,** 69, 78, 85, **127**
Sharet (Shertok), Moshe, **65**
Shazar, Zalman, **65**
Sherman, John, 25
Shields, J. V. A., 42
*Sh'ma*, **86**
Silver, Abba Hillel, **65**
Simons, William H., **105**
Simpson, Louis A. M., 23
Singer, Isaac Bashevis, **65**
Singers, 30
Slepak, Vladimir, 149
Smith, Logan Pearsall, 26
Smyrna, 109
Soboleff, Simon E., **14,** 33, 37, 39, 41, **65,** 72, 74, 75, 76, 77, 78, 79, 80, 81, 82, 84, 85, **105, 116, 120, 138**
Sobremonte, Thomas Trevino de, 147
Social activists, 19, 20, 41, 53, 54, 61, 64
Social workers, 6, 15, 42, 70
Sociologists, 4, 35, 52
Solomon, A. S., 89
Solorzano, Papeles Varios, **147**
Soviet Union, 101, 147. *See also* Russian/Soviet Jewry
Spaatz, Carl, **134**
Spain, 147
Speer, Albert, 144
Spies, 61, 88
Spingarn, Arthur B., **14,** 29, **65,** 66, **132**
Spingarn, Joel E., **66**
Spinoza, Baruch, **66**
Spivak, Lawrence E., **14,** 20, 23, 32, 33, 46, 55, 56, 60, 61, **66,** 67, 69, 71, **105**
Standley, William H., 78
Stanton, Edwin M., 25
Stanton, Elizabeth Cady, 20
Stein, Gertrude, **66**
Steinhardt, Laurence A., **14,** 44, **66,** 68, **106, 120, 138**

Stephens, Alexander H., 25
Stephens, Harold M., 31, 39
Stern, Isaac, **66**
Stokes, Rose Harriet Pastor, **15**
Stone, Harlan Fiske, 29, 30, 31, 39, 48, 54, 57, 76
Stone, Isidore Feinstein, **67**
Storey, Moorfield, 66
Stout, Wesley W., 36, 60
Straus, Michael Wolf, 37
Straus, Oscar S., **15,** 20, 37, 39, 42, 44, 52, 53, 54, 57, 59, 60, 64, **67,** 68, 69, 72, 73, 74, **112, 116, 132, 150**
Strauss, Joseph, **15**
Strauss, Lewis Lichtenstein, **15**
Strauss, Robert S., **67**
Streicher, Julius, 144
Stumpp, Karl, 144
Sudan, 94, 100, 102
Sullivan, Mark, 22
Sulzberger, Arthur Hayes, **68**
Sulzberger, Mayer S., **68**
Sutherland, George, 29
Sweetser, Arthur, 22, 42, 52, 57, **112**
Swing, Raymond G., 34
Syria, 92, 93, 94, 95, 98, 99, 101, 102, 105, 106
Szilard, Leo, **68**
Szold, Henrietta, **68**

Taft, Charles P., 41, 46, 57, **106, 120, 123, 134, 138**
Taft, Robert A., 47, 65, **106, 112, 120, 127, 132, 138, 141**
Taft, William Howard, 20, 22, 29, 31, 39, 52, 53, 54, 57, 58, 59, 61, 63, 64, 67, 68, 70, 72, 81, **106, 112**
Talmadge, Thomas Dewitt, **112**
Taylor, Myron, 42, 57, 72, **116, 132,** 137, **138–139,** 140, **141–142, 146**
Technion, 75
Tel Aviv University, **75**
Teller, Edward, **15, 69**
Terhune, Albert P., **106**
Terrell, Mary Church, 55
Terrett, Colville, **106**
Tewson, William O., 69

Thayer, William S., **106**
Thompson, Huston, 29
Thompson, Jacob, 25
Thyssen, Fritz, 140
Toland, John, **135, 139, 142, 147**
Tolson, Melvin B., 65
Toner, Joseph M., **90**
Touro, Judah, **15**
Touro Synagogue, 89, 91
Trans-Jordan, 98. *See also* Jordan
Traubel, Horace, 20, 45
Trenholm, George A., 25
Trenholm, William L., 49, 73
Trilling, Lionel, **69**
Trotsky, Leon, **69**
Tubian, Henry, 127
Tuchman, Barbara W., **69**
Tucker, Nathaniel B., 25
Tumulty, Joseph P., 42, 52
Tumulty, William, 23
Tunisia, 93, 96, 100
Turkey, 93, 94, 95, 96, 97, 103, 104, 105, **106**, 107, 147, 150
Tyler, John, 25, 58

Union of Orthodox Rabbis, **83**
United Arab Republic, 98, 102, 107
United Jewish Appeal, **84**, 120
United Lubavitcher Yeshivot, **84**
United Nations, **15**, 103, 110, 115, 118, **120**, 131
United Nations Relief and Rehabilitation Administration (UNRRA), 105
United Synagogue of America, **84**
University of Haifa, **75**
Unknown Jewish Martyr, **84**
Untermeyer, Louis, **15, 69**
Uris, Leon M., **69**

Vaad Hatzala Rehabilitation Committee, **84**
Van Buren, Martin, 58
Vandenberg, Hoyt S., 47
Vander Poel, Halsted, 41
Van Devanter, Willis, 29
Van Dorn, Earl, 25
Van Doren, Irita B., 32, 34, 39, 45, 48, 49, 50, 52, 68, 70

Van Loon, Heinrik Willen, 128
Veblen, Oswald, **16**, 28, 34, 37, 59, 70, **139**
Virgin Islands, 137
Von Neumann, John, **16**, 34, 59, 69, **70, 106, 147**
Voska, Emanuel V., **139**
Vrooman, Carl Schurz, 29

Wadsworth Family, 25
Waksman, Selman Abraham, **16**
Wald, Lillian, **70**
Walker, Robert J., 25
Wallace, Henry A., 20, 21, 26, 27, 30, 32, 33, 37, 41, 43, 44, 48, 49, 50, 55, 60, 63, 65, 66, 68, 80, 86
Walsh, David I., 29
Walsh, Thomas J., 23
Warburg, Felix M., **70**
War Crimes and Trials, **139–142**
War Refugee Board, 138
War Relief Control Board, 138, 139
Warren, Charles, 29, 31, 39, **139**
Warren, Earl, 33, 37, 39, 41, 62, **107**, **120**
Warsaw Ghetto, **142**
Washburn, Stanley, 52
Washburne, Elihu B., 25
Washington, Booker T., 20, 42, 62, 64, 70, 72
Washington, George, **91**
Washington, George Theodore, **142**
Washington, George Thomas, **107**
Washington, D.C., 89, 90, 91
Washington Hebrew Congregation, **75, 84,** 89
Waterman, Alan J., 23, 37
Waterman, Alan T., 59
Watterson, Henry, 47, 57
Wayman, Dorothy G., 39
Weinberger, Caspar, **107**
Weiss, Edoardo, 35, 40
Weizmann, Chaim, **70–71**, 114, 116
Weizmann, Ezer, **71**, 105
Weizmann Institute of Science, **75**
Weizmann World Memorial Committee, **84**
Welles, Gideon, 26

Welsh, George P., **107**
West Germany, 118
Wexler, Harry, 70
Wheeler, John H., 26
Wheelock, John H., 55
White, Harry, 23
White, John C., **147**
White, Thomas, **107**
White, William Allen, 29, 31, 33, 36, 37, 39, 42, 50, 52, 57, 58, 62, 67, 68, 69, 72
Whitlock, Brand, 29
Whitman, Walt, **4,** 35
Wicks, Frances G., 63
Wilkinson, Paul, **126**
Willcox, Walter F., 48
Williams, Charl Ormond, 57
Williams, John Sharp, 23
Willis, Edward, 26
Wilson, Edith Bolling, 23, 57
Wilson, James H., 67
Wilson, Woodrow, **16,** 20, 23, 29, 32, 39, 42, 52, 53, 57, 59, 61, 63, 64, 67, 68, 70, 71, 72, 73, 81, **107, 127**
Wise, Isaac Mayer, 88
Wise, Stephen S., **71–72,** 116, 137, 139
Wister, Owen, 48
Wolf, Simon, **16, 72,** 89
Wolman, Abel, **16**
Wolman, Leo, **16**
Woodhead Commission, 111
Woodson, Carter G., 62
Woolley, Robert W., 23, 29, 57, **116**
Works Progress Administration (WPA), 25, 62, **90–91, 106,** 116, 122, 123, **136**
World War I, 95, 98, 99, 106
World War II, 97, 139–142. *See also* Holocaust
World Zionist Organization, 84
Wouk, Herman, **72**
Writers, 3, 4, 5, 7, 9, 13, 17, 21, 32, 36, 45, 47, 49, 53, 54, 59, 60, 62, 64, 65, 66, 69, 72, 73. *See also* Playwrights; Poets
Wunderlich, George M., **16**

Yard, Edward M., **107**
Yemen, 101
Yeshiva University, **76**
Yiddish language, 87, 90, 91
Yom Kippur War, 101
Youth Aliyah, **84**
Yugoslavia, 139, 146
Yulee, David Levy, **73,** 89

Zangwill, Israel, **73**
Zappula, Frank S., **122**
Zeitlin, Jacob, **16**
Zionism, **113–116**
Zionist activists, 2, 4, 5, 28, 32, 36, 37, 42, 52, 53, 54, 56, 58, 68, 70, 71, 73
Zionist Organization of America (ZOA), **85**
Zola, Emile, **17, 73**
Zorach, William, **17**
Zweig, Stefan, **17, 73**

## ABOUT THE COMPILER

Gary J. Kohn was for many years associated with the Manuscripts Division of the Library of Congress. He is now active in the investment field.

Z 6373 .U5 K64 1986
Kohn, Gary J.
The Jewish experience    APR 15 1987